SCOTTISH
COASTAL
STEAMERS

1918-1975

SCOTTISH COASTAL STEAMERS

1918-1975

'The lines that linked the lochs'

Brian Patton

·MARITIME HERITAGE·
from
The NOSTALGIA Collection

First published in June 1996
Reprinted December 1996
Reprinted August 1997
Reprinted in revised format July 1999

British Library Cataloguing in Publication Data

A catalogue record for this book is available from the British Library

ISBN 1 85794 123 3

Silver Link Publishing Ltd
The Trundle
Ringstead Road
Great Addington
Kettering
Northants
NN14 4BW

Tel/Fax: 01536 330588
email: sales@slinkp-p.demon.co.uk

Printed and bound in Great Britain

Unless otherwise stated all photographs are by the author.

SLP

A Silver Link book
from
The NOSTALGIA *Collection*

Half title Three officers of the turbine steamer *Atalanta* photographed on board in 1936, her last year on the Clyde. She was then employed on the Millport service, and in fog on 26 June managed to run aground when approaching the pier. Captain A. Macdonald is on the right, the Chief Engineer is centre and on the left is the Mate, Fergus Murdoch. In post-war years Mr Murdoch went on to win great renown as Captain of *Duchess of Hamilton* from 1946 to 1967. This was the only example in these years of such a long-term partnership, and together master and steamer were an outstandingly successful team. *G. E. Langmuir Collection, courtesy of The Mitchell Library, Glasgow City Libraries*

Frontispiece The 'map of regular passenger services' from the 1954 MacBraynes timetable of Royal Mail services to the Western Highlands and Islands.

Below Norman Wilkinson RI (1871-1965) was educated at Portsmouth School of Art and, perhaps because of this, became a painter who seemed most at home with maritime subjects. In the First World War he worked on the camouflage of ships and afterwards painted many pictures for use as posters by the London & North Western (LNW), London, Midland and Scottish (LMS) and Southern railways. In 1924 he organised an exhibition at the Royal Academy for the LMS, and in the following year that company commissioned this poster of the Clyde. It is hard to pinpoint the exact location, but it is most likely to be from Ashton, to the west of Gourock, looking towards Loch Long, with Kilcreggan and Cove on the right. One of Wilkinson's favourite techniques, when painting a scene with a ship, was to place that ship very firmly in its place in the landscape or seascape. In this he differed from other painters of posters who often exaggerated the size of the ship to the detriment of her surroundings. The steamer in question here is *Duchess of Argyll*. *National Railway Museum, York*

LMS THE FIRTH OF CLYDE
BY NORMAN WILKINSON. R.I.

CONTENTS

CLYDE COAST
Via CRAIGENDORAN
TRAIN and **STEAMER SERVICES**
TOURS and **EXCURSIONS**
JUNE, JULY and AUGUST 1937
LONDON & NORTH EASTERN RAILWAY

INTRODUCTION

The steamers that served the coasts and lochs of Scotland have for generations exercised a fascination for those who have known them far greater than the interest aroused by similar ships elsewhere. Probably this was because they were an integral part of the everyday life of the communities they served. Residents depended on them for most of the basic necessities of life, and visitors could either not have reached their holiday destinations without the steamers, or, having got there, would not have had the chance to enjoy cruises to surrounding beauty spots. It is true that ships on other rivers have been looked on with affection; many Londoners, for example, still cherish happy memories of day trips down the Thames aboard *Royal Eagle* or *Royal Sovereign*, but in relation to the totality of London life, these ships played only a very small part.

It was not so, and to a large extent still is not so, with a community such as Iona. In the past *King George V* was in summer the island's main link with the outside world, and now the car ferry *Lochbuie* fulfils a similar role. In this way the ships became a part of folk memory and, at times, a matter of lively political concern in the affairs of local authorities. Such considerations are not simply a question of the past, as will be apparent to anyone who has followed the history of recent attempts to privatise Caledonian MacBrayne or to introduce Sunday sailings to Lewis and Harris.

It is tempting to see the history of the steamers in terms of a golden age, which is now irretrievably gone. It is true that the range of excursion sailings has been greatly reduced compared to that available even in the 1960s, but in fact the number of passengers carried on the ferries of Caledonian MacBrayne is not far short of totals that were formerly reached, while the number of vehicles is of course far above these. How far the sailings were ever profitable may be doubted, and it is certain that they will always require some amount of public support, but today a service of increased frequencies on almost all routes is provided on a year-round basis, in ships of a standard of comfort undreamed of before 1939. It is, for example, possible that someone relaxing today on *Isle of Lewis* – and this could be someone who is still under 75 – will remember childhood trips on *Glencoe*, sharing the deck with a noisy herd of sheep or cattle. The improvement has been tremendous.

But there can be no doubt that some of the romance has gone. The times when crowds swarmed aboard a steamer at Bridge Wharf to sail down the river and admire Clydeside's latest creations taking shape on the stocks of 20 shipyards, when the holiday masses stormed Wemyss Bay pier on the Saturday of Glasgow Fair, when, lazing on an Arran beach, one could hear from afar the drumming of propellers as *Duchess of Hamilton* made her way up Kilbrannan Sound – all such scenes are firmly in the past.

However, the picture is not all gloom. The preserved *Waverley* and *Balmoral* between them have continued the traditions and, particularly in the West Highlands and on the East Coast, have revived sailings that have been unavailable to the public since 1939, or is some cases 1914; those who maintain these ships deserve heartfelt thanks from enthusiasts and holidaymakers alike. It has been encouraging to note also in recent years the revival of cruising by ships of the Caledonian MacBrayne fleet, both on imaginative special sailings and on a regular basis, and it is gratifying – though disappointing for those left behind – that some such cruises in the year of writing were over-subscribed.

This book is not intended as a general history, but a word or two about the ancestry of the present ships may not be out of place. From the first steamer – Henry Bell's *Comet* of 1812 – ships were owned by private individuals or companies, some of which, such as that of David MacBrayne, became large and important. Although rail/steamer connections were available from the middle of the century and became the main means of reaching coast towns for regular travellers, this form of ownership persisted throughout the 19th century, with the North British Railway (NBR) forming the exception from a very hesitant start in 1866. But in 1889 the Caledonian Railway (CR) and in 1892 the Glasgow & South Western Railway (GSWR) began to operate fleets of steamers on their own behalf, and the days of the private company were numbered. The Caledonian actually did so by its associated Caledonian Steam Packet Company (CSP). This form of organisation proved to be so advantageous that it was retained by the CR's successor, the London, Midland & Scottish Railway (LMS), from the

Grouping of the railways in 1923, and by 1937 all LMS steamers were under CSP ownership. The NBR had a similar organisation, but from 1902 the ships were owned directly by the railway and at the grouping in 1923, without much external sign of change, were transferred to the London & North Eastern Railway (LNER). David MacBrayne passed in 1928 into the joint ownership of the LMS and Coast Lines Ltd. The remaining private operators on the Clyde – Williamson-Buchanan and the Campbeltown Company – were taken over in 1935 and 1937 respectively. Details of these changes are given in the text. The last private company to trade with the West Highlands, MacCallum, Orme & Company, passed to MacBrayne in 1948.

In the brief post-war period before nationalisation the LNER showed commendable

One of the more attractive features of some paddle steamers was the opportunity to stand out on the sponson, by the paddle box, and look ahead to the bow, as the ship made her way along. It could be especially interesting on a day when the sea was choppy, though spectators ran the risk of getting distinctly wet! This view is from the port sponson of the diesel vessel *Talisman* and was taken off Toward when she was employed

on the Sunday winter service in February 1961. This involved a run from Gourock to Rothesay, then across to Fairlie for a train connection for Millport, and for enthusiasts provided a very enjoyable winter cruise. Her use on this route meant that *Talisman* was the last paddle packet steamer, as opposed to car ferry, to operate on a year-round service in British waters. She was finally withdrawn in November 1966.

enterprise, and it is to this that we owe *Waverley*. The CSP, however, as part of the LMS, appeared to be sunk in the dull torpor that had gripped that railway as a whole and made no attempt to take advantage of money that would have been available as compensation for war losses to update its fleet. In 1948 British Railways therefore inherited an ageing and uneconomic fleet. They immediately threw away much goodwill by incredibly crass handling of the question of steamer liveries, insisting that every ship should carry the standard colours, and by an attempt, which backfired, to ban bands on Clyde steamers. When, early in 1952, there was a long-overdue proposal to reduce loss-making services, the public relations aspect of the exercise was so badly handled that it too backfired, and not all the economies could be made, at least at the time.

Neither were local authorities without blame in these years. They fought every small increase in fares tooth and nail, at a time when with rising prosperity and increasing wages these were necessary and would probably not have been noticed by travellers. They even briefly forced the re-introduction of a two-class system on the ships after it had been abolished by BR. The result of this was that, when fares did go up, they had to be increased by a very large percentage. BR became the enemy, with whom war had to be waged. Only in 1952 did BR seem to realise what it was doing, and then instituted a very comprehensive programme of new building and modernisation, which brought to the Clyde the ABC car ferries and 'Maid' Class motor vessels, as well as rejuvenated cruise ships.

The years from 1953 to 1963, with the glorious summers of 1955 and 1959, were the last golden age of the steamers. Restoration of much local control to the CSP also ensured that the image of a remote and uncaring London-based management was dispelled. But by 1963 holiday patterns were beginning to change and, with the drawback of some miserable summers, the losses mounted. Retrenchment of the cruise business began and continued until it was almost extinct by 1981. Even the fine new 'Blue Trains' on the electric lines made little difference by the time they reached Craigendoran, and none at all by the time they reached Gourock. The only bright spot was the growth of car ferry business, to the extent that the ABC ships, only ten years old in 1964, were already obsolete.

Thus the stage was set for the removal of the Clyde ships from railway control in 1969 and the amalgamation with most of the MacBrayne fleet as Caledonian MacBrayne in 1973. But the success story that has followed is outwith the scope of the present book. Rather this is an invitation to remember the steamers as they were before that date and to see how the changes, which have led to the present system, were begun. It is hoped that, in the perusal of this story, memories of holidays and happy days on board, of old friends who carried the freight, who took travellers away and brought them home, whatever the weather, will be rekindled for those who visited the areas they served and for those who lived there.

It would not have been possible to write this book without the help of a great many people. Among library and museum staff, Ms Anne Escott of the Glasgow Room and Ms Moira Thorburn, photographer, of the Mitchell Library in Glasgow have gone to considerable trouble in retrieving and copying items from the collection of the late G. E. Langmuir, and I am most grateful to them for help so readily given over many visits to the Library. I would also like to thank Ms B. Cole of the library, National Railway Museum, York; Mrs V. Boa of the McLean Museum, Greenock; Bill Scott, formerly Local Studies Librarian, and other staff of Argyll & Bute District Council; the staff of the Business Records Department of the University of Glasgow Archives; and the library staff at the headquarters of P&O Ferries, London. From the National Maritime Museum, Greenwich, Messrs D. F. K. Hodge and R. Todd have been most helpful in tracking down photographs of the steamers.

I would also like to mention the following people who have given valued and valuable assistance: Alfred Brown, Carlisle; William Campbell, Isle of Jura; James Craig, Stonehaven; Miss G. Crewe, Bristol; A. Duncan, Gravesend; Mrs C. Fraser, Forres; Hugh Gould, London; Robert Grieves, Paisley; Dr Alasdair C. Harper, Glasgow; Mrs K. Hunter, Arbroath; Miss A. K. James, Edinburgh; Allan Old, Edinburgh; Cliff Parsons, World Ship Society, Manchester; and Sandy Paterson, Glasgow.

A close-up of the paddle box of *Jeanie Deans* as she leaves Rothesay in July 1959.

1. 1919 – DEFINITELY NOT A GOOD YEAR

The first year of peace after the 'Great War' must have been one of the most difficult for steamer operators. The public had an unreasonably high expectation of a return to peacetime standards and naturally wanted to enjoy life, after the horror and privation of the previous four years. Moreover, wages had risen during the war and, as there had been little on which to spend them, many people had much more money in their pockets than ever before. The railways and their own and private operators' ships were, on the other hand, run down, and a battle with the government about compensation was just beginning, at a time when organised labour could no longer be ignored. It was a difficult summer and managers must have been glad when it was over.

The Glasgow & South Western Railway was perhaps best placed, since it had retained *Glen Sannox* on the Clyde from 1915, and its other large paddler *Juno* was returned virtually unscathed early in 1919, taking up service again on 28 June. With the anti-submarine boom removed, there were again through services from Greenock to Rothesay and the Kyles of Bute, and *Juno* spent the season on these rather than her own Ayr excursions. Workmen are seen here putting the finishing touches to her before she resumes service. The GSWR turbine *Atalanta* was also fully reconditioned in time for the July holiday rush. *Glasgow University Archives, McQueen Collection*

Left No other returning war veterans were ready for that summer, and it was necessary to continue to charter a ship that was well past her prime, *Isle of Cumbrae*, chartered from Buchanan Steamers Ltd since 1916. She once again sailed to Rothesay, where she is seen in 1919. She is clearly a very tired old lady by this date! *Glasgow University Archives, McQueen Collection*

Below If life was difficult for the GSWR, it was almost impossible for the Caledonian Steam Packet Company (CSP). Their manager and founder, James Williamson, died in February 1919 and Charles Bremmner took over, although he had at that time no ships to call his own! Even when two were returned, *Duchess of Argyll* and *Marchioness of Breadalbane*, they had to be rushed into service without a complete overhaul. Here again services were maintained only by chartering. One of the ships involved was *Benmore*, the last on the Firth not to have the comfort of a deck saloon. She did her best to cope with the crowds travelling to Rothesay during that summer, but inevitably there were long delays and passengers had to spend hours queuing on Wemyss Bay pier before being able to continue their journey. On a particularly bad day a boy fell between the ship and the pier just after she had arrived from Rothesay, and although he was fortunately fished out unharmed, the accident added to the delay. *Benmore* is seen here off Gourock in 1919. *G. E. Langmuir Collection, courtesy of The Mitchell Library, Glasgow City Libraries*

Above Just when reconditioning should have been going ahead, one of the best remaining ships of the fleet, *Duchess of Rothesay,* was discovered on 28 June 1919 sunk on the bed of the River Clyde at Merklands Wharf. The exact cause of the accident was not established, perhaps because she was still under Admiralty control, but the delay made the CSP's problems worse, and the wreck was also in the way of river traffic. Salvage in the murky waters of the Clyde was not an easy business, but was accomplished by building a coffer dam around the ship and pumping the water out by compressed air, the system being operated with a donkey boiler, seen here on the quay. For some time the *Duchess* appeared to be stuck fast in the mud, but finally she broke the surface and was towed off for a fuller reconditioning than would otherwise have been necessary. A new tea room was fitted during this overhaul, and she returned to service in 1920, apparently, according to newspaper reports, as spick and span as ever and showing no trace of her immersion. *Glasgow University Archives, McQueen Collection*

Right Some of the steamers on war service had to survive very extensive damage. *Mercury* of the GSWR fleet had become a minesweeper and had the misfortune to lose first her stern then, one day after returning to duty at Harwich, her bow; this photograph shows her after the latter incident. She was taken to the Thames where a new bow section was fitted; it must have been something of a temporary measure, since the operation had to be repeated during her post-war refit. Clearly she must have been made of strong stuff to survive such damage, though no doubt it weakened her hull in the long run. *McLean Museum, Inverclyde District Council*

2. THE CLYDE

In Glasgow harbour

In common with almost all other ports, Glasgow has seen enormous changes in the last 30 years, with the decline of shipbuilding and the closure of docks. Much of the area is now almost unrecognisable from the time when the following views were taken in the not-too-distant past.

Associated with this process of decline has been the ending of the cross-river ferries. One of the pleasures of Glasgow harbour for the shipping enthusiast was the network of passenger ferry services which criss-crossed the river. These were provided by the Clyde Navigation Trust under an Act of 1840 and were of course intended to provide transport for local residents and port workers; as they were free within the city boundary, they were also very attractive to local children at weekends and holidays!

The first ferries had been rowing boats, but after an accident at Clyde Street in 1865, when such a boat was swamped and several workmen drowned in the cold darkness of a winter evening, steam vessels were introduced. The design of these did not change greatly over the years, although deck shelters were added after 1945 and a shelter for the helmsman at a later date. Most of the boats were steam-powered and panted energetically as they went about their business, especially when docking; the landing stages were actually flights of stairs, and an incoming boat would bump up several of these before coming to rest. They must have been the only boats anywhere that regularly climbed stairs!

Ferry No 2 is seen here working at Clyde Street in 1966, shortly before that ferry closed. She was one of the first diesel boats, built in 1934, and is wearing the colours of the Clyde Port Authority, which had taken over the services on New Year's Day of that year. She was sold, with other redundant ferries, to the Forth and Clyde Canal Society, but was not used and later scrapped.

Beyond, at Anderston and Lancefield Quays, are two Burns & Laird cross-Channel ships. Nearer is *Lairdsloch* of 1944, which operated on the service to Derry, and beyond her *Royal Ulsterman* on the Belfast service. Both ships became redundant, in 1969 and 1967 respectively, and strangely both met their end as a result of the fighting in the Middle East. *Lairdsloch* had been sold to Israeli interests for use as a water carrier in the Red Sea, under the name of *Hey Daroma*, but shortly after arrival at Eilat she was sunk by Arab commando frogmen. *Royal Ulsterman*, after a spell as an accommodation ship, became the Greek cruise ship *Sounion*, and as such was bombed and sunk at Beirut in 1973.

Right A view from the north bank of the vehicular ferry at Govan in 1954. The Clyde Trust operated these ferries at three points on the river. The first went into service in 1890 and replaced a chain ferry that had become difficult to operate due to the growing harbour traffic. The movable platform on which vehicles, and in some cases passengers, travelled could be raised and lowered by steam to suit the tides. However, the vessel shown here, *Vehicular Ferryboat No 4*, was propelled by diesel-electric machinery, which also operated the platform. She was built in 1938 and, having closed the Govan service in 1965, was withdrawn when the similar service at Finnieston closed early in 1966. To the left of the ferry is Harland & Wolff's Govan shipyard, a branch of the better-known Belfast yard. Today the entire is occupied by low-density housing and looks very different.

Below The ferry between Renfrew and Yoker, the only one still to operate on the Clyde, is of ancient origin, being mentioned in a charter of James VI of 1614. It was operated until 1911 by the Town Council of Renfrew, and was then passed to the Clyde Navigation Trust. In 1936 a new ferry was built for the service, still chain-operated but distinguished by a new livery of blue hull and yellow and black funnels and fitted with enclosed saloons. This vessel carried tremendous traffic during and after the war years; it was used regularly by workers on the Hillington industrial estate and those in the shipyards on the north bank. At peak times a torrent of humanity swarmed ashore as soon as the gates were opened, all, it seemed, bent on catching the first 9 or 26 tram at Yoker or the first 28 at Renfrew.

A new diesel boat was built for the service in 1952. Very early on the morning of New Year's Day 1965 this vessel was discovered in the middle of the river without lights, and for this adventure both the master and the engineer were fined £5 for being drunk in charge of a ferry!

From the mid-1960s traffic declined to under half a million passengers and only 45,000 vehicles in 1983, and it was proposed to close the ferry. However, there was a considerable outcry from many quarters, and instead of closure Strathclyde Regional Council, who had been meeting the deficits, decided to run the service itself with two new ships. This service began in 1984 and has continued since, still meeting a definite transport need in the area.

This view shows the 1936 ferry at Yoker in pre-war days. The then new brick waiting room on the left incorporated the turnstile for fare collection, at that time ½d but raised in the war years to 1d.

From 1926 to 1964 the post of ferrymaster was occupied by Mr Angus Shaw, whose father had held it before him and whose uncle had operated the ferry in the 1890s. Mr Shaw lived in a house just to the right of the ferry slip and was a well-known figure in Yoker, where he was an elder of the parish church and, after retirement, lived long enough to see the new ferries of 1984. The house is now a wine bar.

Above The last cross-river ferry, also of ancient origin, was to be found at Erskine and was acquired from Lord Blantyre by the Clyde Trust in 1904, though not worked by them until 1907. Latterly the service was provided by the ship built for Renfrew in 1936, rebuilt and enlarged to take 20 cars; the flared sponsons were added to maintain stability. This pastoral scene dates from as late as 1967 and there is no great amount of traffic, but in only four years the ferry would be replaced by the present suspension bridge. The boat was not scrapped but instead went back to Renfrew as spare. In 1984 she was acquired by Renfrew Council and fitted out as a museum of local history, as such appearing at the Glasgow Garden Festival of 1988. Unfortunately cuts in local authority funding have, for the time being, brought this initiative to an end and she is at present laid up at Renfrew.

Below left The last of the traditional small ferries to operate was that at Kelvinhaugh, which had at one time performed a triangular run to serve both sides of the entrance to Queen's Dock. The service was withdrawn in October 1980,

following the reopening of the Subway. In March of that year some local boys are enjoying the traditional free sail, while beyond, in dock, is *Manx Viking*, carrying the colours of the then independent Manx Line; she was the first conventional car ferry to serve the Isle of Man, in August 1978, but her entry into service was delayed and her owners were obliged to sell out to a combine of Sealink and James Fisher.

Below right One of the thrills of an 'all the way' trip was seeing new liners under construction, and tremendous interest was shown by the public in *Queen Mary*, which, during her time on the stocks at Clydebank between 1931 and 1934, came to symbolise first the despair then the renewed hope of these depressed years on Clydeside. The huge uncompleted hull of No 534 brooded over the town of Clydebank for several years and could be seen from a considerable distance around, and few were unaware of her presence. When work was resumed early in 1934 there was much rejoicing, and both Williamson-Buchanan Ltd and CSP offered special trips to view the liner. This handbill is for an up-river cruise by *Duchess of Argyll*. *Author's collection*

PLEASE RETAIN THIS BILL FOR REFERENCE

LONDON MIDLAND AND SCOTTISH RAILWAY AND
THE CALEDONIAN STEAM PACKET COMPANY, LTD.   B. 9422 R

Friday, 17th August

Special
Up-River Cruise
To View

No. 534
(THE NEW CUNARDER)

By Turbine Steamer
"DUCHESS OF ARGYLL"

Kilcreggan - -	leave	6.15
Blairmore - -	„	6.30
Dunoon - - -	„	6.45
Gourock - - -	„	7.5
Greenock (Princes Pier) - -	„	7.15

Arriving back at Greenock (Princes Pier) about 15.0, Kilcreggan 16.15,
Blairmore 16.30, Dunoon 16.45, Gourock 11.0 p.m.

FARE	1/9

CONDITIONS OF ISSUE OF EXCURSION TICKETS AND OTHER TICKETS AT LESS
THAN ORDINARY FARE—These Tickets are issued subject to the Notices and Conditions
shown in the Company's Current Time Tables

August, 1934.   J. BALLANTYNE, Chief Officer for Scotland.
B.R.O. 63302.

Above Perhaps because of the growing international tension of the years during which she was built, Queen Elizabeth, No 552, did not attract quite the same public interest as her sister had done. Nonetheless, many people still wanted to see her, and a good crowd aboard Queen-Empress have moved over to the port side as the steamer passes Clydebank in 1938, causing her to list heavily. G. E. Langmuir Collection, courtesy of The Mitchell Library, Glasgow City Libraries

Below The last occasion on which a view of a great liner under construction was possible was during the building of Queen Elizabeth 2 at John Brown's yard in 1967, seen here from Queen Mary II.

'All the way'

The direct sailing from the centre of Glasgow was the traditional method of reaching the coast and went back to the origin of steamer traffic with *Comet* of 1812. The coming of the railway later took away much of the regular traffic, and by the late 1860s passengers for Dunoon, Rothesay and Millport normally travelled via Greenock or Wemyss Bay. But the 'all the way' sailing retained its popularity with tourists, who wanted to see something of the harbour and shipbuilding yards of the second city of the empire, and with poorer people, who found the cheaper fares an advantage and did not mind spending an extra hour on the journey. Piers at Govan, Partick (until 1906) and Renfrew were also easily accessible from nearby tenement housing.

In the 19th century the Clyde often smelled very badly, being virtually an open sewer, but the Glasgow Corporation sewage scheme completed in

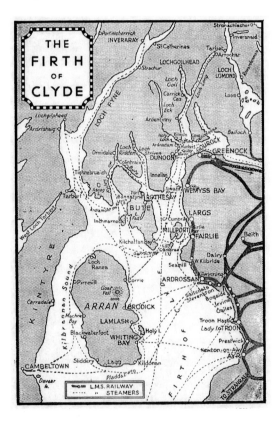

A map of Clyde services in 1939, taken from the LMS/CSP/Williamson-Buchanan Steamers timetable of that year. LNER routes are not shown. *Author's collection*

Right The original terminus for the sailings was on the north bank of the river, at the Broomielaw, the historic heart of the port of Glasgow, and in the 19th century this wharf could be very congested indeed, with up to six steamers alongside at one time. The building of first the railway bridges leading into Central, then, in the 1920s, the George V road bridge curtailed the space available. Here *Isle of Arran*, built for Buchanan in 1892, is about to depart from Glasgow in 1921. She has been somewhat modernised following her successful war service, with the bridge moved forward of the funnel, and is working the 10 am excursion to Dunoon, Rothesay and Largs, with a cruise around Cumbrae. Beyond, *Lord of the Isles* prepares for a cruise round Bute. *G. E. Langmuir Collection, courtesy of The Mitchell Library, Glasgow City Libraries*

1894 removed that nuisance and in the first decade of this century the sailings enjoyed something of a revival. Cargo was also handled, mainly by the MacBrayne and Campbeltown ships but also by John Williamson's *Benmore* and, later, *Kylemore*.

Just after the end of the war, in 1919, the last of these firms merged with Buchanan Steamers Ltd, the main provider of 'all the way' cruises, to form Williamson-Buchanan Steamers Ltd. The Williamson white funnel with black top was chosen as standard for the merged fleet. The services continued to be popular and were improved by the transfer of *King Edward* in 1927 and the building of *Queen Mary*, later to become *Queen Mary II*, in 1933. At the end of the 1935 season the company was taken over by the LMS, who wisely retained it as a separate entity, along with the white funnels for the ships on the Glasgow services.

The separate company was wound up in 1943 and, post-war, the two ships remaining on the 'all the way' service had yellow funnels. After *King Edward* was withdrawn at the end of 1951, *Queen Mary II* sailed alone, with occasional help from

Right Somewhat later in the decade, *Eagle III* of 1910 leaves on the 11 am service to Dunoon, Rothesay and a cruise to the Kyles of Bute. This service was always particularly popular with Glaswegians and many still remember the thrill of setting off for a day out on this ship. One speciality of the 'all the way' ships was the availability of a fare that included meals, making the trip an even greater bargain and also saving the harassed pursers the task of issuing separate travel and meal tickets. In 1933 the fare for this cruise, 'first cabin' with lunch and high tea, was 9s 6d; this compares with a rail/steamer fare of 7 shillings for the cruise to Arran via the Kyles of Bute, with at least a further 6s 6d for meals on board. On the end of the shed are advertisements for Lux soap and Swan Vestas matches, and beyond can be seen the funnel of one of the Burns & Laird Irish ships. *Author's collection*

other ships. But rationalisation meant that she was increasingly needed on other services, and first the Saturday then, incredibly, the Sunday service was abandoned, before all sailings cam to an end after the 1969 season. They have since been revived by *Waverley*, but, with the closure of the yards and docks, much of the interest has gone from the trip 'doon the watter'.

Above In 1929 there was a move to a new terminal on the opposite bank, known as Bridge Wharf (South Side), from which *King Edward* is seen setting off for the coast. Ahead of her is one of the ships of Messrs William Sloan & Company, which provided a service from Glasgow to the Bristol Channel and, until 1932, still carried passengers. The last Sloan ship left Glasgow in 1965 and the company went out of business in 1968. *Author's collection*

Below In the 1930s *King Edward* made a Sunday afternoon trip to Lochgoilhead, leaving Glasgow at 2.15 pm and arriving back at 9.20. As only 35 minutes were allowed on shore at the destination, where the ship is seen in this view, most people went for the pleasure of the sail alone. The fare for the cruise, with high tea, was 5s 6d in what Williamson-Buchanan called 'first cabin'. Tea would have offered a choice of fish, ham and tongue or cold joints with salad and pickle, bread both white and brown, followed by teabread and biscuits, all washed down with cups of tea dispensed by stewards from large silver teapots. For those who felt hungry between times, the tea room offered more of the same, but without the cooked dishes, while fruit and confections were available at the shop on board. *Author's collection*

Above As seating on deck was limited, passengers could hire deck chairs for the day at a charge of 6d, as advertised on the notice at the end of *King Edward*'s upper deck. The chairs consisted of a piece of rug stretched across a wooden frame and were not especially comfortable for a long period; however, they could easily be folded and taken to another part of the deck if the wind shifted round during the cruise. They all carried an abbreviation of the ship's name, such as 'KE', followed by a number. On turbine steamers, rugs could also be hired for 1 shilling per day.

This view dates from the mid-1930s and shows the steamer lying at Rothesay, on her way back from the Kyles of Bute, at around 4.30 pm. Ahead of her is *Glen Rosa*, which would have come from Millport. One of the engineers has taken advantage of the pause to come up for a breather, beneath the upper deck. *Author's collection*

Cal. S.P. Co. Ltd.
Series (A)
Date
Deck Chair Ticket.
Chair No.
CHARGE -/9 Z
Valid Day of Issue Only

Right In 1957 the CSP introduced a cruise up river from coast resorts to Glasgow, to allow visitors staying there a chance to see the river, and it proved to be most popular. It was pioneered by *Marchioness of Graham*, but in later years was undertaken by *Waverley* or *Caledonia*. Having disembarked her passengers, the latter is seen preparing to cant in the river on 28 July 1967, with apparent total disregard for the Clean Air Act, which had already begun to transform the city. Turbine ships turned at the entrance to

the docks and proceeded astern to Bridge Wharf, but paddle steamers, including *Columba*, always canted at their berth.

The cruise started from Largs and picked up passengers at Rothesay and Dunoon, arriving in the city at 1.50 pm. Many passengers would have taken advantage of a sightseeing tour provided by the coaches of W. Alexander & Sons (Midland) Ltd, which awaited the arrival of the steamer at Bridge Wharf and brought passengers back just in time for departure at 4.20. The fare for this, in 1967, was 4s 6d.

Rather strangely, the combined fleet still traded as John Williamson and Co, and the telegraphic address was 'BENMORE', the name of John Williamson's first ship. The timetable for 1934 (*above*) shows the then new *Queen Mary* and also contains details of the sailings to Campbeltown and Inveraray. The company also issued a guide, with maps, a tradition continued by British Railways which, in 1955, replaced the previous rather basic free folder by this attractive brochure (*right*), with detailed maps of each stage of the route. *Queen Mary II* is still the cover ship, but now shares it with one of the new 'Maid' Class motor vessels, which appears to be taking the 'inside' channel at the Narrows in the Kyles of Bute. *Author's collection*

Opposite above The tenements of Govan came right down to the river bank at Govan pier, which was actually situated at the Meadowside passenger ferry. Many local people used this pier, either when going on holiday or having a day trip, since this avoided the added expense of a journey into the city. Already well-laden, *Queen-Empress* calls to pick up more passengers. *G. E. Langmuir Collection, courtesy of The Mitchell Library, Glasgow City Libraries*

Opposite below Isle of Skye, the veteran of the merged fleet in the 1920s, paddles rather slowly downstream in 1924, her normal duty being the 9.30 am departure for Rothesay, from where she returned at 2.30 pm. She had been built in 1886 and was by now decidedly antiquated, but despite this there was a great deal of life left in her and we will meet her again in the section on the East Coast, whither she went when sold in 1927. *Author's collection*

Above A view of *Queen Mary II* passing John Brown's shipyard at Clydebank around 1950; she appears, unusually, to have very few passengers aboard. Built by Denny in 1933 at a cost of almost £62,000, she was not fast but was one of the most spacious and comfortable steamers on the Clyde and a great favourite of Glaswegians. She had more covered accommodation than any other ship and, even when carrying a full complement, did not seem overcrowded. Particularly comfortable was the 1st Class lounge forward on the promenade deck, with spacious settees upholstered in fawn moquette, lit by shaded lamps, and, as a centrepiece, a portrait of HM Queen Mary. This had been presented to Williamson-Buchanan by the Cunard Line, when the former's directors had agreed to alter their new ship's name to allow it to be used for the Cunarder; one wonders what would have happened if they had refused! Below was a spacious dining saloon. Steerage or 'second cabin'

accommodation aft was also a great advance on that provided in other ships. Late in the ship's career the settees were replaced by tip-up seats from a closed Glasgow cinema which, while comfortable enough, completely ruined the appearance of the lounge, and the dining saloon became a cafeteria, being replaced by the 'Queen's Room' on the lower deck forward; this was pleasantly decorated in blue, but there was no view from it whatsoever.

Below In 1954 *Queen Mary II* acquired a mainmast to comply with new regulations, and many thought she was then at her most handsome, with a nicely balanced profile. Here she is approaching Rothesay at 4.40 pm on Sunday 6 June 1954, on the return trip from Tighnabruaich to Glasgow. The pier at Renfrew had been destroyed in the blitz of 1941, while that at Govan was closed after the 1953 season, so the steamer ran from Dunoon direct to Bridge Wharf, arriving at 7.35 pm. By now the return fare to the Kyles of Bute was 10 shillings, and as tickets inclusive of meals had not been reinstated after the war, passengers would have to find another 9s 6d for lunch and high tea. This still had to be booked in advance, this procedure normally requiring a long wait in a queue, and the member of the family detailed to attend to this would not see much of the river above Yoker! However, many would have taken advantage of the 'special new cafeteria service' (as advertised in the timetable) to have a cheaper snack, without the formality of pre-booking and with the added advantage of being able to take food up on deck.

Right Unlike the piers at most resorts, that at Largs was owned by a railway, the LMS, and in the 1930s that company erected at the pier-head a new information and booking office, in a vaguely Art Deco style, which fitted in with other new buildings in the town, such as Nardini's cafe. Unfortunately the effect was spoiled by the clutter of huts that was allowed to remain on the pier. In front of the public conveniences is a lamp post in a much more striking version of the same style. The side of the pier is used for hoardings, advertising (again) Swan Vestas and, in case of 'holiday tummy', Andrews Liver Salts.

This photograph would have been taken just before 2 pm in 1933 or 1934, and *Queen Mary*, still without the suffix, is on her way to cruise to the Arran coast or, if it is a Thursday, to Skipness in Kintyre. The fare from Largs was all of 1s 3d and passengers were back at 4.30. *Author's collection*

Below Apart from the timetabled sailings, 'all the way' trips were very popular with special parties and until after 1960 it was not uncommon for three or four ships to leave Bridge Wharf with these in a single day. For example, the social and recreational associations of the South of Scotland Electricity Board chartered *Duchess of Hamilton* for a day in each of the years 1957-59, the destination varying between Ardrishaig, Tarbert and Lochranza. On Saturday 1 June 1957 the steamer cruised to the first of these. Entertainment on board was provided by an orchestra, with singing and dancing, but in addition other pastimes more normally associated with long-distance cruising, such as deck quoits, pillow fighting and ninepins, were promised. The steamer left Bridge Wharf at 9 am, called at Gourock at 11 and reached Ardrishaig at 2 pm. The return departure was at 4.30 pm prompt (excursionists were warned to leave ample time to return on board) and, again with a call at Gourock, arrival in the city was at 8.50. The actual route was to be set according to weather conditions.

Lunch was served in four sittings, beginning at 11 am, and tea similarly, beginning on departure from Ardrishaig. As passengers' meal tickets specified both the sitting and the saloon, the auxiliary dining saloon on the lower deck must have been in use. At Ardrishaig the local bowling green was open to the party and, if the weather had been inclement (it was in fact dry, but dull), the public hall would have been made available for an impromptu dance. Groups who wished to see something of the countryside could hire one of the coaches that awaited *Duchess of Hamilton* at the pier.

Charter rates were very low; in 1954 a turbine steamer cost £370 per day, less 7% commission in certain cases, and a motor vessel was only £100 for an afternoon or evening. However, the outings must have demanded a good deal of organisation, both on the part of the associations and of the officers and crews of the ships.

This view shows *Duchess of Montrose* leaving Glasgow with a charter in the later 1950s. In the middle of the river one of the dredgers of the Clyde Navigation Trust is hard at work, attended by *Hopper No 7*, while *Royal Scotsman* and a Burns & Laird cargo motorship - *Lairds Moor* or *Lairds Ben* of 1948 - lies at the terminal on the north bank. *G. E. Langmuir Collection, courtesy of The Mitchell Library, Glasgow City Libraries*

The 'Royal Route'

The mail service operated David MacBrayne Ltd from Glasgow to Ardrishaig and, as the ship's destination boards proudly proclaimed, 'Oban and The North' had been advertised under the above title since the late 19th century. The name was based, somewhat tenuously, on the journey made by Queen Victoria in *Sunbeam*, one of the company's predecessor's track boats, along the length of the Crinan Canal in 1847. In fact, although complimentary about the furnishings of the boat, the Queen found the passage 'tedious' and, having reached the sea at Crinan, Her Majesty immediately boarded the (first) *Victoria and Albert* to resume her travels independently, although she did use the canal again on the return journey; apparently this time it was less tedious. Years later, in 1873, she sailed on *Gondolier* from Banavie to Inverness. But even if royalty had generally preferred the seclusion of its own yacht, the publicity value of the 'Royal Route' slogan was too good to miss – there was no need to mention what the Queen had actually thought of

THE ROYAL ROUTE . THE ISLES OF YOUTH

SEE THIS **SCOTLAND** FIRST

it – and it was used extensively until the service came to an end in 1970.

In the 20th century, the steamers associated with the first leg of the route from Glasgow (Gourock in post-1945 years) to Ardrishaig were *Iona, Columba, Saint Columba* and *Lochfyne* in summer, and *Grenadier* and later *Lochfyne* in winter, although of course other ships sailed on the route from time to time. Until 1910 the departure time from Glasgow was 7 am, but after several changes and the interruption caused by war, it settled down in 1924 to the famous timing of 7.11 am, at which it remained until 4 September 1939.

Breakfast was served as soon as the steamer left Glasgow. The MacBrayne guide book for 1936 points out that 'This is no common ordinance. It is a meal of circumstance and you are poorly equipped for humane encounter and cheerful

things if you do not remember it and speak about it. A great epicure, Colonel Newnham Davies, has commended the breakfast herring, placing them high on the list of the world's famous dishes'.

No doubt passengers who had risen early were glad of the herring, and the guide book helpfully assured travellers that, for the convenience of tourists, a speciality was made of hot breakfasts, which were served on all the steamers after leaving port in the morning. The charge for the meal, in 1936, was 3 or 2 shillings in 1st Class and 2s 6d or 2 shillings in 3rd. Class distinction persisted with MacBrayne for some years after it was abolished on other Clyde steamers, and the guide warned sternly that 3rd Class passengers found using the Saloons for any purpose whatever would be charged the 1st Class fare; pursers applied this rule zealously and any encounter along these lines was not likely to be especially humane!

Iona and *Columba*, unusually, together in the river at Glasgow in the 1920s. *Columba* lies alongside one of the quays on the north bank, while *Iona* is manoeuvring in the middle of the river. The most likely date for this view would be 1922, when *Iona* was employed on a service from Glasgow to Lochgoilhead. On the right at Windmillcroft Quay lies *Ballycotton* of the

Clyde Shipping Company, one of the oldest established firms in the steamship business, whose ships sailed from Glasgow to Waterford and Cork and from Glasgow to London with intermediate calls. Passengers were carried on many sailings until 1939, the cheap fares and good food making these trips most popular, with a regular clientele. *Author's collection*

Above In September 1956 *Saint Columba* sweeps majestically into Dunoon on the return journey from Ardrishaig.

Left After 1958, when she was on the run both summer and winter, *Lochfyne* was normally relieved for overhaul by *Lochnevis* in April and May. Here the latter arrives at Dunoon in May 1959.

Above From time to time *King George V* acted as a relief steamer on the 'Royal Route', the last period being in the autumn of 1960, when *Lochfyne* was required for the Islay route in place of *Lochiel*, which had grounded in West Loch Tarbert, with rather serious consequences. The Clyde can be an ugly sea in winter, and on 2 November 1960 Rothesay was to be the last port of call at which the steamer was able to uplift any passengers. Inellan and Dunoon were out of action due to a combination of a high tide and a strong north-easterly gale, though *KGV* did come close enough to the latter to allow the postal staff to throw the mailbags aboard, and Gourock was likewise closed to shipping. The voyage terminated, somewhat late, at Custom House Quay, Greenock, then not normally used by passenger ships.

Right Even in 1952 the arrival of the Royal Mail steamer at Rothesay gave rise to a bustling activity, greater than with any other ship. *Saint Columba* lies alongside in August of that year on her way north. From the foremast proudly fly the name and Royal Mail pennants, and Captain MacLean surveys the scene from the wing of the bridge. Most passengers line the rail to watch the activity, but a few remain in their deckchairs to listen to the band, a member of which can be seen beside the third (dummy) funnel.

The rivals: races between *Columba* and the Inveraray steamer *Lord of the Isles (II)* in the years from 1891 to 1912 were a regular thrill for passengers travelling through the Kyles of Bute and in Loch Fyne. Though the speeds were less hectic, racing continued into the 1950s, the main contestants by then being *Saint Columba* and either *Duchess of Montrose* or *Duchess of Hamilton*. The latter could always give the MacBrayne ship a good run for her money, but until converted for oil burning in 1957, the former had little chance of holding off *Saint Columba*, although 18 years her junior. Nonetheless, Archie Campbell, her Captain from 1946 until the end of the 1951 season, was always game to try. At this period, *Saint Columba* was commanded by Captain Robert M. Maclean DSC. (The DSC had been awarded for services at Dunkirk where, with *King George V*, he had made five trips to the harbour and brought out thousands of troops.) Having thus seen off the Germans, he was not inclined to let the railway ships have the upper hand on the Clyde, and in this he was fully supported by Chief Engineer Alex Pinkerton, who was adept at getting that extra knot out of 40-year-old turbines. Sometimes, in the heat of the action, *Saint Columba* would briefly vibrate like one of the motorships. These three views show what invariably happened, seen from the deck of *Saint Columba*.

On Monday 16 July 1951 the two steamers met when the *Montrose* was sailing to Arran via the Kyles of Bute, with a departure time from Rothesay of 10.25, 5 minutes ahead of her rival. In the first view it is clear that her stokers are working hard to build up speed as she heads out of Rothesay.

However, by the time she is off Ardbeg Point, *Saint Columba* has almost closed the gap and her bow is level with the *Duchess*'s midships; the stokers are still doing their best and, no doubt, cursing the quality of coal with which they were supplied in the early post-war years.

By the time *Saint Columba* is entering the Kyles, off Ardmaleish Point, the unequal contest is over and she sweeps proudly past, to berth at Tighnabruaich, the next pier, comfortably ahead of her rival.

Above 'The joy of travelling,' according to the 1934 guide, 'is in going round corners. I must remind you of this, for you are about to enter the Kyles of Bute.' *Saint Columba* is framed by the trees at Rhubaan Point as she speeds away from Tighnabruaich between 1936 and 1939. *Author's collection*

Below In the early 1920s, aviation was a novelty and aerial photography an even newer attraction. No doubt using surplus ex-RAF machines, several enterprising photographers visited the Clyde area to record resorts and steamers from above. *Columba* is seen here, taken from what must have been a very low-flying aircraft! The ship is dressed overall, but it is unfortunately not possible to make out the signal flags. *Author's collection*

Left The magnificent oscillating cylinder engine of *Columba*. It ran at 40 rpm and the sight of the huge cranks swaying back and forward was impressive. That apart, the engine room was cramped and the shaft to the paddle wheels set so high that several steps were needed in the alleyway to allow passengers to climb over it; until a small electric light plant was fitted in 1929, the whole area was also very dark. Such machinery was designed to use cheap coal and by the 1930s was hopelessly uneconomic; on her round trip *Columba* could get through 18 to 20 tons per day. The engine did, however, have the advantage of being smooth in operation, an important consideration for a ship that was designed to carry an exclusive clientele. *Author's collection*

Below left A view of the fore deck of *Columba*, looking aft from the bow. The plank was used to slide luggage down from the promenade deck, and a stout cabin trunk, labelled 'T' for Tarbert, can be seen by the mast. At peak holiday periods *Columba* carried vast amounts of luggage, ranging from the elegant cabin trunks of wealthy English tourists to wee tin boxes belonging to Glasgow Highlanders going home for the Fair; but Lachie, the baggage man in the 1920s, was more than equal to handling all of these. The date of the photograph would seem to be the late 1920s and the location is probably the Kyles of Bute. *McLean Museum and Art Gallery, Inverclyde District Council*

Opposite above Tarbert was described by the guide as having a fine natural harbour, and a town built on herring when herring meant money. It was also the point at which passengers for Gigha, Islay and Jura left the steamer at the pier in the East Loch and made their way across to the West Loch to board the vessel that would take them to these destinations, while in the 1930s and post-war years passengers for the 'Tour Kintyre' boarded a coach, operated originally by Craig, latterly by West Coast Motors ('Red and Cream coaches, the symbol of safety, comfort and reliability'), for Campbeltown. Although this transfer traffic has vanished with the Loch Fyne herring, the harbour remains busy and in 1994

saw the inauguration of Caledonian MacBrayne's newest Clyde ferry service to Portavadie on the other side of the loch.

The pier at Tarbert was built in 1879 for the use of *Columba*, since her great length (301 feet) prevented her from using the harbour proper - it was in fact often called the 'Columba pier', to distinguish it from the harbour. To small boys it was always a source of surprise that a ship so large as *Saint Columba* could sweep round the tight confines of the East Loch and tie up at such a small pier, but the manoeuvre was executed daily without mishap. The ship is seen here at the pier in the years immediately before 1939. A half-cab single-decker of West Coast Motors awaits Campbeltown passengers on the right, while in the centre of the picture two smaller buses provide local connections, including that to the Islay steamer. *Author's collection*

Above right Ardrishaig was the terminus of the first part of the 'Royal Route', and after a very brief stay the Clyde steamer would be on her way back to Gourock and Glasgow at 1 pm. By the 1930s those who wished to make a circular tour, the 'Tour Argyll' (fare 12 shillings), could return to Glasgow by 'Luxury Coach', leaving Ardrishaig at 2.30 or 4.34 pm; the road journey was very slightly longer than the rail/steamer service, and required just over 4¼ hours, with arrival in the city timed to the minute, at 6.48 or 8.53.

For many years passengers going north had a choice of route; they could board the small steamer *Linnet* on the Crinan Canal, or they could travel by coach to Ford on Loch Awe, from which another small ship, the *Lochawe*, would take them the length of the loch to connect with a train for Oban at Loch Awe Pier station. This latter route was somewhat slower and, coming south, it was not possible to complete the Oban-Glasgow journey in a day; travellers could, however, say in compensation that they had been to New York, since *Lochawe* called at that tiny hamlet! The latter service was not offered after 1914, and in 1929 a direct motor coach from Ardrishaig to Oban replaced both the *Linnet* and the Crinan-Oban steamer.

An early attempt to gain a share of the lucrative tourist traffic had been made in 1866 by the North British Railway when it operated a rival service to the 'Royal Route', from a base at Helensburgh. The service was a failure and was withdrawn after one season, but it marked the beginning of the association of that railway with Clyde steamer operation, and it was thus commemorated by a special sailing of *Waverley* on 15 April 1966. The ship, dressed overall, is returning to Ardrishaig after a cruise on Loch Fyne.

Above *Linnet* has been likened to a small marine tram and it seems incredible that she could have absorbed the crowds disembarking from the much larger mail steamer in the height of summer. Her actual capacity was 270, and at busy periods the Canal icebreaker was hired to accommodate the overflow. The trip across the isthmus to Crinan involved negotiating 13 sets of locks and required 2 hours. The little ship is seen here at Cairnbaan; passengers could go ashore while *Linnet* negotiated the locks, and the Cairnbaan Stores enjoyed a brisk trade in, among other souvenirs, postcards such as this. *Author's collection*

Below left For many years the service northwards from Crinan was provided by *Chevalier* of 1866, seen here at sea at an unknown date. In 1936 the 'motor car' from Ardrishaig arrived in Oban at 3.20 pm, and here passengers going further north had to spend the night.

Again a circular tour was offered for day trippers, who could catch a train from Oban just after 6 pm and be back in Glasgow by 10.44 pm. The fare for the 'Tour Majestic', 3rd Class rail, 1st on the steamer, was exactly £1. En route passengers could enjoy a meal in a Pullman car, although after 1934 these were owned directly by the LMS, and those travelling 1st Class could view the sunset (rain in Glen Ogle permitting) from the comfort of the observation car 'Maid of Morvern', built for the service in 1914.

There was no lack of hotels in Oban from which to choose. Passengers could opt for the Great Western, the first hotel in the town to be built for tourists, where they could meet those who had chosen to come by road and leave their car in one of the 60 spaces in the garage, or they might have preferred the Park Hotel, with its interior sprung mattresses in the bedrooms. Those with more frugal, or more abstemious, tastes could book in to the Mart Temperance Hotel, where the charge for bed and breakfast was 6 shillings per night. In these days of multi-digit telephone numbers, it is interesting to note that those of the first two were Oban 4 and 5 respectively. At the present time, a reasonable minimum charge for B&B in the area would be £20. If the evening proved wet, the Cinema House in George Street, continuous performance 6.30 pm to 10.30 pm, could provide a welcome diversion. *Author's collection*

Above By 1936 a connecting service to Inverness by the Caledonian Canal, named the 'Wonder Waterway Tour', was provided on Tuesday, Thursday and Saturday only; a connection by steamer and coach was available on other days. From 1928 to 1935 *Iona* provided the link to Fort William, after which year *Lochfyne* took over until 1938; in the last year of peace, the brand new *Lochiel* was on the run. Her first port of call was at the island of Lismore, at 9.10, and here she is seen coming alongside the pier. Lismore is no longer served by large ships, but enjoys two ferry services, for passengers and vehicles from Oban and for passengers only from Port Appin. *Author's collection*

Below Further north, *Fusilier*, which provided the service before 1928, paddles along Loch Linnhe, with the hills of Morvern behind. The view dates from the years after 1926, when the ship was rebuilt and the bridge moved forward of the funnel. *Author's collection*

Passengers on the 'Royal Route' arrived at Fort William at 10.55, to catch a train for the short run to Banavie, the guide book reassuringly pointing out that it was 'just a step' to the train. More recently, rebuilding of the station on a different site has made this a very long step, although few steamers now call at Fort William anyway.

Having been commendably restrained about the Kyles of Bute, the author of the 1936 guide let himself be carried away by the beauty of one of the new motor coaches: 'A MacBrayne coach is like a modern parlour; walnut, cedar and kindly springs . . . inviting as your favourite chair'. The coaches were certainly comfortable, but he omitted to say that the roads in the area were still somewhat primitive, and would remain so until well after 1945. The illustration shows three post-war MacBrayne Maudslay coaches at Fort William pier around 1950, collecting passengers who have just disembarked from King George V. *Robert Grieves Collection*

Right Having got as far as Fort
William, honesty compelled the author
of the guide to mention that most
common phenomenon of the West of
Scotland - rain. However, suggestions
of day after day of continuous
downpour would not have reassured
prospective tourists, and the reference
was both brief and poetic: 'A drift of
rain from Glen Loy passes like a
jewelled curtain . . . and lifts away to
the west, looking like a petal of shining
cloud in the garden of the sky'. Clearly
nothing to worry about!

A regular summer service was
maintained until 1974, in May of
which year *King George V* is moored
alongside the pier, prior to working a
cruise to the Isles of the Sea and
Corrievrechan whirlpool on the
following day. KGV was withdrawn at the end of the 1974
season and this attractive excursion was allowed to lapse.

Below 'It is unusual,' the guide book said, 'to see a scarlet
funnel set in a mass of hawthorn and briar rose.' It went on to
compare *Gondolier*, to which the red funnel belonged, to a toy
ship '. . . able and apt for a voyage away from the shape and
umbrage of the ordinary'. She was, in fact, a fairly substantial
paddle steamer of just under 150 feet in length, and the only
unusual features of her design were the bow and stern, the
former being distinctly canoe-shaped to facilitate handling at
the locks on the Caledonian Canal. Built in 1866, she sailed

between Banavie and Inverness until 1939, when her career
ended as a block ship at Scapa Flow. During the entire inter-
war period she was commanded by Captain Peter Grant. In
1936 she boasted new steel saloons, with picture windows and
a new deckhouse, and it seemed that she would go on for many
years. She is seen here in Loch Lochy in her last years; a
competitor, in the form of a motor car, lurks by the roadside.

It was from this ship in 1934 that the Loch Ness Monster
was spotted 'passing between the bridge stanchions at a speed
of fully 9 knots' and obligingly remaining in view for 10
minutes; in 1936 the MacBrayne guide recommended
tourists to have a camera ready. *Author's collection*

Finally, the tourists reached Inverness harbour at 6.30 pm, where they would be met by buses and porters from the Caledonian, Columba and Waverley Hotels. Those of a temperance disposition, perhaps combined with an interest in fishing, would have made for the second of these, although they would have found hot and cold running water in 'most' bedrooms only; those who wanted to be sure of this facility, or even accommodation en suite, would have made for the first named, which also boasted a 'smart, new lounge', central heating and an 'elevator'. These hotels were reticent about their actual charges, but the Queensgate mentioned that its charges were 'quite modest', The County Hotel, at the high

season, charged 10 shillings per day or 60 shillings per week for full board, while B&B could be had for 7s 6d and 45 shillings respectively. 'And what more fitting end to our journey,' the guide book asked, 'than the citadel with a paring of moon drifting among the chimneys and towers of this restful town?' The photograph shows *Gondolier* alongside at Inverness in the late 1930s.

Passengers could of course return to Glasgow or Edinburgh direct by rail, but both the LMS and LNER offered a wide range of circular tours, allowing visitors to see as much as possible on their return trip. It was, for example, possible to proceed by train to Aberdeen and Ballater, thence by coach to Perth via Braemar and finally by train to the starting point; the tour fare, 3rd Class rail, Cabin on the steamers, was 72s 6d.

Sailings on the Caledonian Canal were not resumed by MacBrayne ships after 1945, although the company did consider the idea and even went as far as surveying the piers. It was not until 1960 that it was again possible to sail on Loch Ness on a regular basis. In that year the British Waterways Board had the tug/icebreaker *Scot II* of 1931, converted to carry passengers, the steam machinery being replaced by diesel at the same time. She is still popular with tourists. *Author's collection*

The coming of the car ferry

The geography of the Clyde Coast does not lend itself to communication by road. Quite apart from the various islands, which must depend on access by sea, towns such as Dunoon and Tarbert can only

be reached by road after a long and, until recent times, uncomfortable journey. Even today, after many improvements, most traffic to the Cowal area still travels by ferry, since an easy drive from Glasgow to Gourock, followed by a 15-20-minute sail, is preferable to an 80-mile slog by road.

Opposite page At holiday times, passengers' luggage in advance added to the chaos. Until after 1960 many families rented a house 'at the Coast' for a month, and for this brought not only their own clothes and holiday gear, but also table and bed linen, all packed in trunks or hampers and, in the case of the better off or better organised, dispatched several days before the holiday began. The charge for this by LNER steamers in 1937 was 2 shillings per item including collection, conveyance and delivery, or 1 shilling for conveyance with either collection or delivery, while the LMS rates were 1s 6d and 1 shilling. Passengers bound for Dunoon were warned that at that resort delivery was charged to the hotel, and they must make sure that they did not pay the extra 6d.

All this luggage was manhandled on and off the steamers on iron-wheeled barrows over a pair of planks, which, at a low or high tide, could assume a very acute angle relative to the deck. Other families brought their hamper with them when they travelled on the Saturday and handled it themselves. The effect on timekeeping was such that timetables carried footnotes indicating trains - usually commuter expresses such as the 5.13 pm from Glasgow

Central to Wemyss Bay - that would not carry passengers' luggage, or from which luggage would not be forwarded by the connecting steamer. Surprisingly the trunks almost always reached their correct destination in time, and the railways did not share the reputation of some present-day airlines for losing baggage.

These two photographs give an idea of how luggage was handled. In the first, taken at Whiting Bay, *Duchess of Montrose* is berthed outside *Glen Sannox* at the pier, and everything has to be taken across her deck before being landed. One crewman is struggling with a number of metal buckets tied together, while beyond him another carries some kind of wooden object on his shoulder. The junior purser looks on with some concern, after checking the tickets of two passengers. On the after deck of the *Sannox*, the seats have been rearranged to leave space for cars, and the rear of a Ford Consul can just be seen. The seamen's jerseys carry the letters 'BR'; these would revert to 'CSP' some years later.

In the second photograph, luggage is brought ashore from *Duchess of Montrose* at Brodick on 27 June 1952, in a very labour-intensive manner. One man pulls a barrow with three cabin trunks, while a second follows with a suitcase and what might be a tent under his arm. On the pier, a third crewman is returning a bicycle to its no doubt relieved owner, while a man in a trilby hat checks his luggage. A worried-looking boy in a gaberdine coat watches the operation. Behind the gangways and rowing boat on the pier are a pile of trunks and more bicycles, Arran being then an excellent place for cycling. Meanwhile, the galley boy has taken time of from peeling potatoes to chat to one of the pier staff. *World Ship Society, George Osbon*

Above It was not only luggage that was a problem. Vast amounts of deck cargo were also carried, in the form of all sorts of goods for the daily needs of the local communities. For example, during the Second World War Millport was bread-less until *Marchioness of Graham* arrived on the first down run of the day. Most MacBrayne ships were designed to carry both passengers and cargo, the handling of the latter usually dictating the timetable. Here cargo is winched off *Claymore* of 1955 at Tiree in 1973. Again the number of crew required can be seen; this particular operation evidently required the attention of four people.

Below Milk churns, full or empty, each proudly emblazoned with the farmer's and farm's name, were another source of delay, though when empty they could be rolled down the planks at low tide. Here milk churns are manhandled ashore from *Waverley* at Rothesay in June 1969. By this time most such traffic went by road tanker in the car ferries, and this must have been a somewhat exceptional occurrence.

Carriages had been carried by steamers in the 19th century - there is a photograph of *Benmore* with two on her deck - and cars since early in the present century, but shipment involved all concerned in a somewhat hazardous operation. Cars could be taken only at or near high tide and were driven on and off the steamers over two planks; it was clearly impossible to ship vehicles if the weather was anything but flat calm. Until the late 1930s the steamers had little space in which to stow motor vehicles, and it was, for example, almost impossible to get anything larger than a motor cycle on board *Queen Mary II*. However, *Marchioness of Graham* of 1936 and *Juno* and *Jupiter* of the following year had large clear areas amidships and could take up to six cars. During the war years the after decks of many of the turbine steamers were cleared of seats and used for cars and cargo, and when peace returned *Duchess of Argyll* retained this arrangement, allowing her to take up to ten cars. Commercial vehicles were difficult and double-decker buses impossible; when these were used on Bute after 1943, they were taken to the island by landing craft.

In the first photograph the proud owner of what would appear to be a nearly new Morris 1000 coaxes the car over the planks as he drives off *Talisman* at Wemyss Bay in 1959. Behind, crew members prepare to manoeuvre the luggage barrows on to the pier - part of the pile of trunks can just be seen to the right of the car.

In the second view another Morris Minor, new in 1956, is craned ashore from *Lochnevis* at Armadale two years later, to the relief of the owners. *Author/S. M. McCulloch*

Top In 1949 the loss-making cargo services of Clyde and Campbeltown Shipping Company Ltd were taken over by the British Transport Commission, under the management of the Railway Executive. They were ultimately transferred to the CSP, which thus became even more aware of the problem of providing the Clyde area with an effective cargo distribution service. The ships actually involved in the work in 1949 were all coal-fired steamers, *Ardyne*, *Minard* and *Arran*. However, the services to Dunoon and Campbeltown ceased immediately, leaving only those from Glasgow to Rothesay and Ardrossan to Brodick and Millport.

For years one of the most familiar ships on the Clyde was *Minard Castle*, though few tourists ever trod her decks. She had been built in 1882 for the Lochfyne & Glasgow Steam Packet Company, whose founders were merchants in the Loch Fyne area who were dissatisfied with the MacBrayne services. Until 1926 she plied between Glasgow and Inveraray, calling at many small piers that were bypassed by the Turbine Steamers vessels. She carried both cargo and passengers, but for the latter the accommodation was basic. She has a place in literature, as she figures occasionally in Neil Munro's 'Para Handy' stories. In this view she is lying across the eastern end of Rothesay pier in 1919. *Glasgow University Archives, McQueen Collection*

Middle *Minard* had been built in 1906, in part replacement for *Minard Castle*, although with rather less and even more basic passenger facilities. These remained available to the public until the end, although they were not advertised in post-war years. She worked on the Loch Fyne service until it was discontinued in 1949, and was then placed on the direct cargo run from Glasgow to Rothesay. She is seen here at the latter port on 17 August 1954, just six weeks before the service ended; it is around 10.30 am and in the morning rush-hour the cruise ships take precedence.

Bottom The pier of Colintraive in the eastern Kyles of Bute did not at any time enjoy a particularly good service, and cruise ships bypassed it altogether. It was, however, one of the piers to which passengers might have travelled by cargo steamer. Around 1930 either *Minard* or her near sister *Ardyne* is at the pier, which finally closed in 1946. *Author's collection*

As well as cars and people, agricultural produce, especially livestock, was shipped by passenger steamer. The sponson area of a paddle steamer could easily be roped off, but it was more difficult on a turbine, and a passenger who carelessly opened the door from a deckhouse could find himself in the middle of a flock of sheep. The noise and smell could be trying, and further time would be lost after the four-footed passengers disembarked as the crew made the steamer fit for human occupation again. Bulls were especially difficult. In the first photograph the Purser of *Duchess of Fife* contemplates a flock of sheep disembarking via the passenger gangway. Calves normally travelled tied up in a sack, as seen in the second picture on the foredeck of *Glen Sannox* of 1925 en route from Arran to the mainland in August 1953. G. E. *Langmuir Collection, courtesy of The Mitchell Library, Glasgow City Libraries/Author*

Naturally the railway companies were aware of the drawbacks of this state of affairs. The LMS did not say much about it, but in 1937 the CSP ships carried over 1,000 cars to or from Dunoon. The LNER, in its timetable for 1937, gave rates for conveyance of cars from Craigendoran to Dunoon, Rothesay or Largs; cars up to 10 cwt cost 10 shillings per single journey, then the rates went up by weight to 22s 6d for anything over 25 cwt. To put this into perspective, it should be noted that a day return from Glasgow to Rothesay, 3rd Class and Saloon, was 4 shillings.

However, spurred on by a question in the House of Commons and being about to introduce a car ferry from Stranraer to Larne, the LMS asked the CSP to prepare a report on the topic, and this was duly received in February 1939. It was suggested that a new vessel be built for a service between Gourock and Hunter's Quay and that slips be constructed at these terminals. By the time shipyards were asked to tender for the new ferry, it had been decided to use existing piers and that the ship would accordingly have to be fitted with a lift. In view of the progress of the diesel engine, and its success in ships of the MacBrayne fleet, it is surprising to read in the *Dunoon Observer* of 1 April that a steamer to carry 20 cars was to be ordered, and there is no reason to think that this was an April Fool! There were further changes, and in the end a fairly basic design was chosen, offering little accommodation for passengers; it was evident that the ship was seen as an addition to the fleet and not as a replacement for one of the ferry paddle steamers. However, the outbreak of war put an end to these plans and the ship was not built.

Finally, in 1951 Lord Hurcomb announced that the British Transport Commission, which was now thoroughly worried about the losses being sustained on the Clyde, was to spend £1 million on the upgrading of services. Three of the new vessels would be general-purpose ships, with a capacity of 500 passengers, around 26 cars, livestock and 50 tons of general cargo. They would be fitted with electric lifts and ramps to allow them to operate to any pier and at any state of the tide. The first ship to be launched was *Arran*, built by Denny, the steamer *Arran* being then renamed *Kildonan*. While she was running trials in December 1953, she went to the assistance of *Caledonia*, which had broken down. The other two ferries, *Bute* and *Cowal*, were built by the Ailsa Shipbuilding Company at Troon.

On the misty and very cold morning of 4 January 1954, *Arran* waits at Gourock pier prior to making the first car ferry sailing to Dunoon.

Above The first car is driven on board, watched rather apprehensively by the crew who, at that time, had not yet developed their later expertise at handling this kind of traffic. *Arran* left at 12.10 pm with 12 cars and over 300 passengers.

Right When *Arran* arrived at Dunoon, reported the *Evening Times*, she was greeted by a large crowd, encouraged, no doubt, by the wintry sunshine that had meanwhile broken through. As a special concession no pier dues were charged on this occasion. Welcoming Lord Inverclyde and the various visitors, Miss C. S. McPhail, Chair of the Pier Committee of Dunoon Town Council, said that the inauguration of the vehicle ferry service was an important event in the history of the Clyde. Dunoon had had a ferry service of this kind in mind for many years and now, thanks to the progressive policy of the British Transport Commission, the desire for that was today being realised. Lord Inverclyde then cut a white ribbon to allow the first car off the ferry, seen here. This was driven by A. K. Stevenson, Secretary of the RSAC, with passengers D. Stewart of the RAC and J. Lindsay of the AA. The distinguished guests then adjourned for lunch.

Left A view of *Arran* alongside at Dunoon later in the day.

Below Finally, in July 1957, Arran at last got its dedicated car ferry, and it seemed that she had been worth waiting for. The order again went to the Ailsa Company at Troon. Not only was *Glen Sannox* able to take many more cars than the older trio (over 40, depending on size), but her passenger accommodation was much more spacious and she was faster, being capable of 18 knots. Arran folk and the many visitors to the island took her to their hearts and were sorry to see her removed to other services in 1970. She is seen here alongside Brodick pier in May 1961.

Top and middle The new service was brilliantly successful and, despite an indifferent summer, 10,000 cars had been carried by mid-July. Part of the reason for this success had been the reduction in fares and the introduction of return fares for cars, at one and a half times the single fare, but in part it was also due to the quickly acquired skills of the crews at handling cars on board and the captains at handling the new ships. *Arran* had been brought into service by Captain A. Purves and he was soon joined by Captains W. Smith and J. MacLeod.

The service to Rothesay was inaugurated by *Cowal* on 1 October 1954, but it was soon evident that all three ships - *Bute* having been delivered soon after - would be needed on these two routes and that Arran would have to wait. The timetables of 1954 and 1960 reproduced here show how the services developed. *Author's collection*

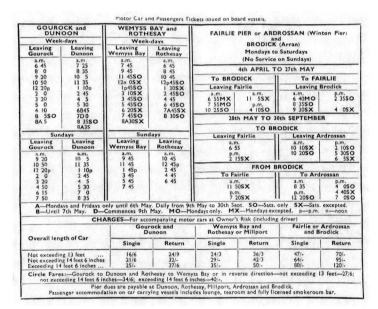

SERVICES

GOUROCK TO DUNOON					DUNOON TO GOUROCK			
Leaving Gourock					Leaving Dunoon			
MONDAYS TO FRIDAYS					MONDAYS TO FRIDAYS			
a.m. 6 45	a.m. 10 50	p.m. 2A0	p.m. 6 10		a.m. 7 28	a.m. 11 35	p.m. 1B35	p.m. 5 30
8 5	p.m.	3 5	8A5		8 35	p.m.	2A35	6 45
9 20	12 10	5 0	—		10 5	1A10	3 35	8A35
SATURDAYS					SATURDAYS			
a.m. 6 45	a.m. 10 50	p.m. 2 0	p.m. 6 10		a.m. 7 28	a.m. 11 35	p.m. 2 35	p.m. 6 45
8 5	p.m.	3 5	8 5		8 35	p.m.	3 35	8 35
9 20	12 10	5 0	—		10 5	12 35	5 30	—
SUNDAYS					SUNDAYS			
a.m. 10 0	p.m. 12 40	p.m. 4 25			a.m. 10 30	p.m. 1 15	p.m. 5 5	
11 15	2 5	5 40			11 55	2 40	6 20	
—	3 15	7 5				3 50	7 55	

A—Commences 31st May.   B—Ceases after 28th May.

Motor Car and Passengers Tickets issued on board vessels.

GOUROCK and DUNOON		WEMYSS BAY and ROTHESAY		FAIRLIE PIER or ARDROSSAN (Winton Pier) and BRODICK (Arran) Mondays to Saturdays (No Service on Sundays)				
Week-days		Week-days						
Leaving Gourock	Leaving Dunoon	Leaving Wemyss Bay	Leaving Rothesay					
a.m. 6 45	a.m. 7 25	a.m. 7 45	a.m. 6 45	**4th APRIL to 27th MAY**				
8 0	8 35	9 45	8 45	To BRODICK		To FAIRLIE		
9 20	10 5	11 45SO	10 45	Leaving Fairlie		Leaving Brodick		
10 50	11 35	12n 0SX	12p45SO	a.m. 6 55MX	a.m. 11 5SX	a.m. 6 40MO	p.m. 2 35SO	
12 20p	1 10p	1p45SO	1 30SX	7 55MO	p.m.	8 35SO		
2 0	2 45	3 10SX	2 45SO	10 25SO	4 10SO	9 30SX	4 0SX	
3 20	4 5	3 45SO	4 45	**28th MAY to 30th SEPTEMBER**				
5 0	5 30	5 45SO	6 45SO					
6 10	6B45	6 20SX	7A45SX	To BRODICK				
8 5SO	7D0	7 45SO	8 30SO	Leaving Fairlie		Leaving Ardrossan		
8A 5	8 35SO	8A30SX		a.m. 6 55	a.m. 10 10SX	p.m. 2 10SO		
	8A35			10 20SO	5 30SO			
Sundays		Sundays		2 15SX	6 5SX			
Leaving Gourock	Leaving Dunoon	Leaving Wemyss Bay	Leaving Rothesay	FROM BRODICK				
a.m. 9 20	a.m. 10 5	a.m. 9 45	a.m. 10 45	To Fairlie		To Ardrossan		
10 50	11 35	11 45	12 45p	a.m. 11 50SX	a.m. 8 35	p.m. 4 0SO		
12 20p	1 10p	1 45p	2 45	p.m.	p.m.	4 40SX		
2 0	2 45	3 45	4 45	7 20SX	12 20SO	7 0SO		
3 20	4 5	5 45	6 45					
4 50	5 30	7 45						
6 15	7 0							
7 50	8 35							

A—Mondays and Fridays only until 6th May. Daily from 9th May to 30th Sept. SO—Sats. only SX—Sats. excepted.
B—Until 7th May. D—Commences 9th May. MO—Mondays only. MX—Mondays excepted. p—p.m. n—noon

CHARGES—For accompanying motor cars at Owner's Risk (including driver)						
Overall length of Car	Gourock and Dunoon		Wemyss Bay and Rothesay or Millport		Fairlie or Ardrossan and Brodick	
	Single	Return	Single	Return	Single	Return
Not exceeding 13 feet ...	16/6	24/9	24/3	36/3	47/-	70/-
Not exceeding 14 feet 6 inches	21/6	32/-	29/-	42/3	64/-	95/-
Exceeding 14 feet 6 inches ...	25/-	37/6	35/-	50/-	80/-	120/-

Circle Fares:—Gourock to Dunoon and Rothesay to Wemyss Bay or in reverse direction—not exceeding 13 feet—27/6; not exceeding 14 feet 6 inches—34/6; exceeding 14 feet 6 inches—40/-.
Pier dues are payable at Dunoon, Rothesay, Millport, Ardrossan and Brodick.
Passenger accommodation on car carrying vessels includes lounge, tearoom and fully licensed smokeroom bar.

Bottom The other three ferries, which had become known as the 'ABCs', from the initials of their names, settled down to serving Wemyss Bay-Rothesay and Gourock-Dunoon, with thrice-weekly sorties to Millport. Still in original condition, *Bute* approaches Gourock on an August evening in 1958. Experience soon showed that the facility for general cargo was seldom required and that for livestock 'on the hoof' not at all, as it was much easier to transport animals in road vehicles. During the following winter, therefore, all three 'ABC' ships had the 'goalpost' mainmasts and derrick replaced by a tripod mast, and the hatchway on the poop was plated over. These alterations allowed them to carry about eight more cars, but unfortunately, as the original lifts remained, delays at piers increased. The change also improved the ships' appearance.

Colintraive was not allowed to remain a sleepy backwater for long after the closure of its pier. Just four years later, in July 1950, a ferry was started across the Kyle to Rhubodach on Bute by the Bute Ferry Company, using a converted landing craft. This service thrived and, when larger vessels were required, was taken over by the CSP on Hogmanay 1969. Today ships of the 'Loch' Class are employed, and *Loch Riddon* is seen here from Rhubodach in September 1995.

Naturally the success of the Clyde car ferries was noticed in the West Highlands, and there was considerable public agitation for a similar service to be provided by MacBrayne. The financial implications were considerable, not least because the institution of car ferries would require the rebuilding of many piers and the construction of a new one, at Craignure on Mull. Improvements would also have to be made to many roads. Finally, in 1960 the Highlands & Islands Shipping Services Act allowed the Secretary of State for Scotland to build new car ferries and charter these to David MacBrayne Ltd. The routes were to be Oban-Craignure, Mallaig-Armadale and Uig to Tarbert and Lochmaddy. It took some years to prepare for the new services, and the then Secretary of State had to fight a rearguard action with HM Treasury, whose advisers thought that two ships would suffice to run the three services. Perhaps they were not clear where the ports concerned actually were! The services began in 1964, when *Hebrides*, *Clansman* and finally *Columba* arrived from their builders, Hall, Russell & Company in Aberdeen.

MACBRAYNES

Above It had originally been proposed that the new ships would be painted as on the cover of this brochure announcing the services, with white paint carried down to promenade deck level, and they would have looked good in this colour scheme. When they entered service, however, the black paint of the hull was carried one strake higher. *Author's collection*

Right The start of the Oban-Craignure service was announced for the beginning of May 1964, but unfortunately *Columba* was not ready and the veteran *Lochearn* had to be pressed into service, in a laudable but vain attempt to run to the timetable for the new ship. With crane loading it was impossible, although matters improved slightly when her sister *Lochmor* joined her in June. Here a van is lifted from *Lochearn* on to the new pier at Craignure in May 1964.

Finally on 30 July *Columba* arrived and the service proper could start.
She is shown leaving Oban on a typically wet day in May 1965.

Arran via the Kyles of Bute

'The Royal Route to the Island of Arran is universally conceded to be the finest excursion on the Clyde.' So, in a handbill of 1889, the Frith of Clyde (sic) Steam Packet Company staked its claim to be the premier operator on the Firth. While the statement that it was the finest excursion could be questioned, there is no doubt that, for almost a century, this was one of the most popular trips on the Clyde. It was pioneered in 1880 by a company known as the Frith of Clyde Steam Packet Company, who had built for the service the steamer *Ivanhoe*. The main aim of the enterprise was to run a ship on teetotal lines, to avoid the rowdiness that was often encountered on board steamers at that time, but the success of *Ivanhoe* was probably due in equal measure to the pleasure of travelling on a well-run ship, and it was the patronage of the growing middle class as much as that of the temperance lobby that brought profit to the promoters.

With a crew attired in yachting uniform and extensive floral decorations in the saloons, *Ivanhoe* brought a wholly new concept of service to the Arran route and far out-classed *Scotia*, built in the same year, which maintained the connection via Ardrossan. The attempt to publicise the service as the 'Royal Route', based on patronage of the ship by the King of Saxony in 1886, was a cheeky challenge to MacBrayne but, perhaps because he was regarded as only minor royalty, the slogan did not catch on and its use remained the prerogative of the older firm.

Ivanhoe had always been worked closely with the Caledonian Railway and, from 1889, with the CSP, and in 1897 she was taken over by the latter, bringing to an end the teetotal experiment. The main reason for the take-over was competition from the Glasgow & South Western, which had placed first *Neptune* then the new paddler *Jupiter* on the same route. *Ivanhoe* was then replaced on it by the almost new and much speedier *Duchess of Rothesay*, which was, along with *Duchess of Argyll*, to remain associated with Arran via the Kyles of

Bute until 1939. The new *Caledonia* of 1934 also had spells of duty on the service in pre- and post-war days, sharing it then with *Duchess of Montrose*, and the last steamer to provide the excursion was *Queen Mary II*.

Scenically the trip was magnificent. From Rothesay the route lay through the Kyles, with a call at Tighnabruaich, then via the west coast of Bute to Corrie in Arran. There being no pier there, passengers were landed and embarked by a large ferryboat, the timetable stating that this was subject to weather conditions and sufficient accommodation in the boat. The manoeuvres of this ferry always attracted a crowd of interested spectators, both on the ship and ashore. The steamer then proceeded to Brodick, Lamlash and Whiting Bay, where, from the 1920s onwards, she

lay for an hour or so before retracing her route to Corrie. From there the route was by the east coast of Bute and Kilchattan Bay to Rothesay and so back to base. In 1930 the cost of the entire trip from Glasgow, 3rd Class rail, Saloon on the steamer, was 7 shillings.

The ferry at Corrie did not resume operation after the Second World War, and in the last years, when the southern Arran piers had been closed, a cruise to Pladda via the Holy Isle was substituted. Interestingly, a cruise from the upper firth to Arran has been revived by Caledonian MacBrayne in recent years, although the ship does not sail via the Kyles, and in 1995 demand for it often outstripped the capacity of the ferry *Pioneer*. However, few motorists took advantage of the Rothesay-Arran link and it has now been discontinued.

By the First World War *Ivanhoe* had come very far down in the world, having changed owners several times, being used for short 'all the way' trips in the years prior to 1914, and passing in that year into the control of Turbine Steamers Ltd. During the war she was chartered back to her former Caledonian owners, and is seen here on ferry duties at Dunoon in 1919. Mainly she sailed from Greenock and Gourock to Dunoon and the Holy Loch, but she finished her Clyde service on the Rothesay run in August 1919. She was scrapped in the following year. *Glasgow University Archives, McQueen Collection*

Above One of the attractions of sailing on the CSP paddle steamers was that passengers were allowed on to the sponsons, something not possible on most LNER ships. This view of the Narrows in the Kyles of Bute was taken from such a position on *Caledonia* en route to Arran in August 1967. The passage of a large steamer through such a narrow stretch of water never fails to attract interest on board.

Left The view from the main deck of *Caledonia* looking forward as she crosses to Arran on the same day; the view was taken as the ship approached Corrie, and Holy Isle is visible beyond.

Right Duchess of Argyll looms large above the ferryboat at Corrie as she returns northwards at 3 pm on an afternoon in the summer of 1919. The CSP was very short of steamers in that year, and she had somewhat hastily been returned to service on 31 May, as heavy traffic was expected and, in the event, carried on all services. People were glad to relax again after the horrors of the previous four years and the weather also played its part by remaining very fine until mid-August. *Duchess of Argyll* sailed first to Rothesay and resumed the Arran excursion on 1 July.

Before returning to service, she had been inspected by George Erskine, Principal Surveyor of the Board of Trade in Glasgow, and in a letter to the London office he stated that the ship had clearly withstood the strains of war service very well. The only problem area was the forecastle, which had been 'flattened slightly' in a heavy sea; as the ship had been built with an open foredeck, this no doubt accounted for some weakness in that area. Temporary strengthening had been fitted and it was intended at the end of the season to lift the deck, renew the beams and fit larger bracket heel plates. Despite this, he had no hesitation in granting a certificate for the summer, a decision that no doubt brought great relief to the CSP management. She was fully overhauled by Scott of Greenock in the spring of 1920 at a cost of £5,000. *Author's collection*

Below On the outward journey, Corrie was reached at 12.05 pm. Carefully assisted by a crew member, a lady passenger in a cloche hat negotiates the descent from *Duchess of Argyll* into the ferryboat in 1927. From the bridge, Captain James Riddell supervises the operation. *Dr P. Ransome-Wallis, National Maritime Museum, London*

Above A group of interested spectators watch from the seats at the Ferry Rock, Corrie, as *Duchess of Rothesay* prepares to land her passengers. Her funnel wears the yellow/red/black colour scheme adopted by the LMS for the years 1923/24 and known on the Clyde as the 'tartan lums'; in response to much criticism, the red band was dropped in 1925. *Author's collection*

Below A group of passengers sun themselves on the after deck of *Duchess of Argyll* somewhere off the Arran coast in 1922, her last year of operation under the Caledonian Railway. At this time the steamer, particularly when under the command of Captain John McNaughton (from 1919 to 1924), seemed to be in her prime, none the worse for her wartime service. *National Maritime Museum, London*

Above Duchess of Argyll comes alongside Brodick pier in the early 1930s, after her upper deck had been extended aft to give improved accommodation. The card was posted on 14 September 1935 and the writer referred enthusiastically to 'having a good time, a full boat and nice company'. The area to the right of the pier later became the bus stand and is now used to marshall vehicles awaiting the car ferry. *Author's collection*

Below Not many passengers have remained aboard *Caledonia* for the Pladda cruise, for which she is leaving Brodick in 1965. The majority have been attracted ashore either by the chance to visit Brodick Castle, open to the public from 1 to 5 pm, or to enjoy one of the coach tours that had been developed first in the 1930s. That usually advertised in connection with

the Kyles of Bute sailing was Tour No 10C, which ran between Brodick and Lochranza, thus allowing passengers to pick up the Campbeltown steamer on her homeward run - the tour could also be made in the reverse direction. Tours 10A and 10B were circular tours of the island, from Brodick and Lochranza respectively, and 10D was a circular drive around north Arran from Brodick; the extra charge in 1967 for 10C was 4 shillings, and for 10D 6 shillings, and tickets were obtained on board the steamers. Later a circular drive around the southern part of the island was added as Tour 10E. The fare from Glasgow for the sail to Arran was now 21 shillings.

The ship now wears the blue hull colour scheme introduced in that year for ships of British Railways, but, in common with all the Clyde fleet, retains her yellow funnel, with the addition of a lion rampant.

Girvan and Ailsa Craig

While cruises round Ailsa Craig had been operated from an early date, the chance to land on a small and relatively remote island is one that has always appealed to people, and holidaymakers at the resort of Girvan on the Ayrshire coast have for generations taken advantage of its position to sail out and land on the Craig. To cater for this traffic, which was maintained by sailing boats, Mr A. Girvan of Girvan had built in 1906 the small steamer *Ailsa*, which proved very popular on the run. A tea room was built on the island and was well patronised by excursionists, there being little else to do once one had arrived other than walk around on very hard granite!

The entrance to the harbour at Girvan has a very pronounced bar, and even the motor vessel *Lady Ailsa* could often be felt to bump across it when passing in or out. This naturally restricted calls by large ships, and the resort did not enjoy a regular service. Between the wars calls were made by *Juno* and later *Duchess of Hamilton* from Ayr, and *Jeanie Deans* called on some of her long trips between 1932 and 1937. Another fairly frequent visitor was *Queen-Empress* of the Williamson-Buchanan fleet, seen here in the harbour around 1932. No sailings were made for many years after 1945, but calls have been resumed by *Waverley* in recent times, these usually being combined with a cruise around the 'stupendous natural curiosity'. *G. E. Langmuir Collection, courtesy of The Mitchell Library, Glasgow City Libraries*

The Lady Ailsa arriving at Ailsa Craig.

Above Ailsa was replaced in 1924 by *Ailsa II*, soon renamed *Lady Ailsa*. She was a larger ship, almost double the tonnage of her predecessor, and was built at Ayr by the Ailsa Shipbuilding Company; unusually for a Clyde steamer, her engines were made in Aberdeen, by A. Hall & Co. In the photograph she is approaching the fairly substantial pier that was built on the island for her use. Unfortunately the economic depression reduced the profitability of the service and Mr Girvan decided to sell *Lady Ailsa* in 1932, and for a couple of years no sailings were available. In 1934 a motor vessel, also named *Lady Ailsa*, was placed in service. *Author's collection*

Right The motor vessel of 1934 was replaced in 1955 by another, very similar in design to a fishing boat and run by Mr I. Girvan, the grandson of the founder of the service. In this view taken at Ailsa Craig on 10 August 1959, she is the light-coloured boat next to the jetty, which she shares with two fishing boats. The line of rails are part of a tramway that extended some way round the island and was used to transport granite down to the jetty for shipment; this trade has now ceased.

The Campbeltown run

In the 19th century the town of Campbeltown at the end of the Kintyre peninsula was a thriving port and industrial centre, with a population of almost 10,000. One of the local industries was coal-mining, and in connection with this Scotland's only narrow gauge passenger railway, the Campbeltown & Machrihanish Light Railway, was opened in 1903. That apart, the town depended almost entirely on the sea for communication; Glasgow is almost 140 miles distant and even today it is difficult to make the journey in less than 4 hours. Until the late 1930s, road transport was unattractive for passengers and totally impracticable for goods traffic.

When the advantages of steamships became established, a group of Campbeltown merchants and residents formed in 1826 the Campbeltown & Glasgow Steam Packet Joint Stock Company Ltd. For many years this company traded with three ships, but by 1920 the fleet was reduced to *Kinloch* and *Davaar*. The former was sold in 1926 and replaced by the handsome and speedy *Dalriada*,

with which the company re-entered the day excursion market. Road and air transport began to make inroads into profits in the 1930s, and in 1937 the C&G was taken over by Clyde Cargo Steamers Ltd, a subsidiary of MacBrayne, and renamed Clyde & Campbeltown Shipping Co Ltd. The passenger service ended on 16 March 1940 and, as neither ship survived the Second World War, it was not resumed after 1945, while the cargo service finished in 1949.

The company was very firmly based in Kintyre and in the years before 1939 provided a daily service to link the area with Glasgow. The general practice was to have departures from Campbeltown around 7 am and from Greenock at 9 am, although increased services were given at times such as Glasgow Fair. On Mondays a special early run was given for the benefit of returning weekenders, leaving Campbeltown at 4.45 am, passengers arriving in the city at 9.21. For cargo, the steamers proceeded to and from Glasgow, where they latterly berthed at the Broomielaw alongside the Irish steamers, immediately downstream from the new George V bridge.

Kinloch **at Campbeltown shortly before her withdrawal.** *Author's collection*

A view of *Davaar* of 1885, as rebuilt in 1903, alongside at Campbeltown. The saloon and promenade deck above it were reserved for passengers, but in the other quarters, passengers and deck cargo were usually mixed and, at sale times, it was common for every available inch of space to be filled with sheep going for auction. *Author's collection*

R.M.S. "DALRIADA" LEAVING CAMPBELTOWN, EARLY MORNING.

The early Monday service, sometimes known as the 'death run', could not have been a very attractive proposition for passengers, although they were perhaps consoled by the splendour of dawn breaking over Campbeltown Loch, as seen in this view of *Dalriada* leaving Kintyre for Greenock and Glasgow. The excellence of the bacon and eggs served for breakfast on the company's ships no doubt also helped. *Author's collection*

Weather permitting, and it generally did, the ships called off the small village of Saddell, where passengers and cargo were ferried in a large rowing boat, manned by Lachie the ferryman. Again, sheep were commonly handled here, but in this picture, taken around 1930, only a group of lady passengers, who appear to be enjoying the experience, occupy the boat. Their luggage can be seen forward and, among the cargo, is a large box containing tins of Jaap's Health Salts; Jaap was a Glasgow pharmacist and his Health Salts were widely used in the west of Scotland as an alternative to Andrews Liver Salts. *Author's collection*

The next village on the east side of Kintyre is Carradale, which first acquired a pier in 1858. In 1870 that structure was replaced by a new one, which, unusually for the Clyde, was constructed of cast iron rather than wood. Depending on the length of time taken at Saddell, steamers reached here about an hour after leaving Campbeltown, and for many years formed the main means of communication between the two. This photograph shows *Davaar* alongside at Carradale in August 1924. There would appear to be a great deal of luggage and cargo, but not many passengers! Note the gentleman sporting fashionable plus-fours and a deerstalker hat. *National Maritime Museum, London*

Above From Lochranza the steamers proceeded direct to Gourock and Greenock to discharge passengers, before sailing up river to berth in the heart of Glasgow. Here in the late 1930s *Davaar* shares the Broomielaw with the new Burns & Laird motorship *Royal Scotsman*, introduced on the Glasgow-Belfast overnight service in 1936 and providing a standard of comfort and design not before seen on cross-Channel services from the Clyde. *Author's collection*

Below The Campbeltown Company provided a wide range of excursion sailings, aimed to attract local people rather than tourists, and there were also occasional trips from Stranraer to Kintyre. This photograph, taken in 1935, shows *Dalriada* at anchor off Inveraray and may well have been taken on the day of the local Highland Games. Next to *Dalriada* is *Duchess of Hamilton*, which would have brought excursionists from Ayr and Troon, while further offshore *King George V* appears to be getting steam up for her return sailing to Greenock. A handsome motor yacht completes the picture. *Author's collection*

From 1901 until 1935 the summer service from the upper firth to Kintyre was in the hands of Turbine Steamers Ltd; in the latter year it passed to the Caledonian Steam Packet Company. In the early years *King Edward* shared the route with the first *Queen Alexandra*, but after 1920 the second steamer of that name was the regular ship, relieved occasionally by *King Edward* or *King George V* after 1926, and by the paddle steamer *Queen-Empress* at the end of the season in September; when she was on the service, timings had to be eased considerably.

The LMS guide for 1939 stated that the sail to Campbeltown was considered part of the holiday, although passengers who had experienced a Force 8 in Kilbrannan Sound would probably have dissented. Perhaps afraid that the place sounded just too remote, the guide went on to reassure potential visitors that letters and newspapers arrived daily. (There was in fact by this date an air service from Renfrew.) The CSP used *Duchess of Argyll* on the Campbeltown run in the years before 1939, and *Duchess of Hamilton* from 1946 to 1970, although the *Montrose* was seen fairly often in later years, while *Queen Mary II* maintained the service until her withdrawal in 1978.

Between 1936 and 1939 the CSP also offered a fast direct service from Ardrossan, normally by *Glen Sannox* of 1925. Today the only steamer to call is *Waverley*, although proposals, often aired in the past, for a car ferry service, may yet come to fruition.

Neither the date nor the publisher of this engaging piece of 'knocking copy' have been recorded, although it may be assumed that Turbine Steamers Ltd was not sorry to have the superiority of its steamers proclaimed in this way! No doubt the company fondly hoped that no one would remember that one of its turbine services, to Campbeltown, was regularly turned over to a paddler for some weeks in September every season!

The sentiments are only partly true. Although all the early turbines, with the exception of the GSWR's *Atalanta*, were fine sea boats - as was proved by the voyage of *Queen Alexandra* (1902) round Cape Horn on her way to British Columbia and by *King Edward*'s survival of a terrible storm on her return voyage from the White Sea in 1919 - they could still roll heavily enough to upset passengers when rounding Ardlamont Point or going down Kilbrannan Sound in a south-westerly gale. But somehow a sleek turbine looked more stable than a paddle steamer, and there was no harm in cashing in on appearances! *Author's collection*

ERCHIE: "I DAE WISH I HAD TA'EN TONAL'S ADVICE AN' GAED BY TURBINE!"

TONAL: MAN, THIS IS GRAN'! I WUNNER HOO ERCHIE IS."

Before the season began, the excursion steamers went into dock for overhaul and repainting. In this photograph, taken in 1921 or 1922, *Queen Alexandra* of 1912 is in the dry dock of James Lamont & Co, Greenock. Sharing the dock with her is one of the 'puffers' of the Ross & Marshall fleet, whose red/white/black funnel colouring was identical to that of the North British Railway's ships. Outside the dock lies *Queen-Empress*, whose overhaul is clearly further advanced, and behind her one of the handsome tugs of Messrs Steel & Bennie and another 'puffer', Just visible beyond the latter, in the somewhat polluted waters of the West Harbour, is *Benmore*, laid up since damaged by fire in 1920. The harbour was filled in in the autumn of 1923 and the old ship removed to the scrapyard. There is little sign of mechanisation in the shipyard, nor of motor traffic outside, but a handsome white carthorse can be seen on the edge of the dock to the right. *McLean Museum & Art Gallery, Inverclyde District Council*

Above Although the Turbine service was closely connected with the Glasgow & South Western Railway and Princes Pier, Greenock, the ships also called at the Caledonian Railway's piers of Gourock and Wemyss Bay - 'a little sunshine haven' according to the Turbine guide - and in this view *Queen Alexandra* of 1912 is seen at the latter, either just before or immediately after the First World War. It is not clear if the car has come down the pier for shipment to Kintyre - which the guide book called 'Cantyre' - or simply to bring passengers to the steamer. Beyond the car can be seen the railway-style semaphore signals that controlled steamer movements at this busy terminal.

Leaving Wemyss Bay at 9.50 am (in 1935), the steamer then made for the former GSWR railhead at Fairlie, where she was timed to depart at 10.03 - until well into British Railways days, certain steamer services were timed to the minute! It was here that the bulk of passengers for Lochranza

and Campbeltown embarked, having come from Glasgow St Enoch station by the 9.12 express. The up working in the evening was much slower, like many trains from Fairlie, and required 73 minutes to reach the city. Fairlie Pier had been built in 1802, and although it attracted favourable notices when opened, it was not modernised in any way in later years and compared very badly with the rebuilt Caledonian pier at Wemyss Bay. Few mourned when the pier closed in 1972. *Author's collection*

Below The CSP instituted a daily call at Keppel Pier, Millport, and thereafter the next port of call was Lochranza, where *Duchess of Hamilton* is seen framed between two coaches of Lennox Transport Ltd, awaiting circular tour passengers some time between 1965 and 1968. The coach on the left is a Bedford, that on the right an Albion, and both carry Duple bodywork. *Robert Grieves*

Above From Lochranza it was a sail of 30 minutes to the ferry at Pirnmill. It is the late 1920s, and the second *Queen Alexandra* is seen calling. The ladies are fashionable in cloche hats and the age of the motor car has arrived, but the arrival of the steamer still attracts spectators. The CSP did not deign to call here when it took over in 1936, and all services to Pirnmill ceased in 1940 when *Davaar* made the last call. *Author's collection*

Below At one time the turbine ships had called also at Machrie Bay, to the south of Pirnmill, but after 1920 they made direct for Campbeltown, to arrive at 1 pm. On what is evidently a hot and sunny day, in the mid-1920s, the arrival of *Queen Alexandra* has brought a large crowd to the harbour. Among the crowd would be the Boots from the Royal Hotel, a First Class Tourist and Family Hotel ('Boots attend all steamers'). This hotel offered the luxury of private sitting rooms or suites and, by 1931, would also be advertising cars for hire. Advertisements also mention that the business incorporated a funeral undertaker - all eventualities were clearly considered! *Author's collection*

Above This view, taken between 1932 and 1935, shows *Queen Alexandra* coming alongside. She has been modified by the enclosure of part of the promenade deck to give more sheltered accommodation - and, no doubt, to avoid unfavourable comparisons with her consort *King George V*, which introduced this feature to the Clyde in 1926. *Author's collection*

Below 'To many who sail to Campbeltown,' said the guide published by Turbine Steamers Ltd, 'the promise of a visit to the far-famed golfing resort of Machrihanish is of paramount importance. A light railway links the two centres, and trains await the coming of the steamer. Further, it is possible for tourists making the one-day trip to visit Machrihanish and be in no danger of missing the boat home. If there is any likelihood of such a contretemps, it lies in the temptation to stay for a longer spell at this golfing paradise.'

The 'Turbine Express' of the light railway is shown in this early postcard issued on board *Queen Alexandra* (1902). By 1935 the excursion was made by bus, but, as only 40 minutes could be spent at the destination 'on the Shores of the Atlantic', there was insufficient time to do much more than contemplate the ocean. But it sounded so adventurous! *Author's collection*

T. S. Queen Alexandra   Turbine Express

On Board Turbine Steamer King Edward or Queen Alexandra

Steamer & Pier, Campbeltown.

Above In September *Queen-Empress* took over the service and is seen preparing for departure from Campbeltown harbour. Although she was so much slower than the turbine, the schedule was adjusted to allow passengers the same amount of time on shore. Her visits to Kintyre obviously did not generate the same amount of interest as did those of the turbine steamer, and only a few people have gathered to see her off, some time in the 1920s. *G. E. Langmuir Collection, courtesy of The Mitchell Library, Glasgow City Libraries*

Below On the first Friday in June, the date of the Kintyre Agricultural Show, departure from Campbeltown was considerably later than usual, a tradition that was maintained as long as the service lasted. On 1 June 1973 *Queen Mary II* provides the connection and blows off steam shortly after her arrival. In the inner harbour is *Sound of Islay* of Western Ferries, which at that time provided a vehicle ferry service to Red Bay on the Antrim coast of Ireland. This operated from 1970 to the end of the summer season in 1973, and *Sound of Islay* of 1968, Western Ferries' first ship, was re-registered at Campbeltown for this run. Despite her minimal passenger accommodation, she seemed to be successful, but the operation was killed by the Irish troubles. However, since 1997 a service has once again been operated by the Argyll & Antrim Steam Packet Co, using the former Caledonian MacBrayne ferry *Claymore*.

Left In the 1960s the Sunday excursion to Campbeltown was arranged to give a cruise round Arran, the steamer calling at Lochranza on the outward run and Brodick homeward. On a Sunday in August 1964, *Duchess of Montrose* provided the cruise and encountered some rough weather as she came out of Campbeltown Loch on her return trip. *Hugh Gould*

Below The Caledonian MacBrayne ferry *Loch Tarbert* clears the end of the former pier at Lochranza en route to Claonaig in August 1995.

Resorts: Rothesay, Dunoon and Millport

The resort of **Rothesay** could claim with some justification to be the oldest on the Firth, since it had been a summer haunt of the Stuart kings from the 14th century onwards. Its development in the 19th century was at first more industrial than recreational, but from the 1840s it became one of the principal destinations of Glasgow holidaymakers. Queen Victoria visited it in 1847 and referred to it as a 'pretty little town . . . with a fine harbour'. Workers from the industrial belt followed her in their thousands, and its heyday was probably in the first decade of this century. Thereafter it went into a decline, very slowly at first, then accelerating at an alarming rate from 1960 onwards. Only recently have its fortunes begun to turn again, but the days when Argyle Street, Rothesay, could be as busy on a Saturday night as Argyle Street, Glasgow, have gone for ever.

The main problem for Rothesay was that visitors who wished to go anywhere else had to rely on the steamers, and the town was not able, because of its geography, to take advantage of the growth of motor transport until the car ferries arrived in the 1950s. Even then, those who did bring a car found that there were not very many places to go, and bus tours were limited to variations on the 'Round Bute' theme.

In the late 1920s 74 hotels and boarding houses advertised in the local holiday guide, while there were also 61 'apartments', some of which offered attendance and some simply a roof over one's

A poster issued by the LNER for Rothesay, probably between 1925 and 1930, and executed by Fred Taylor (1875-1963), who was employed by both the LNER and London Transport as a poster artist. He had been educated at Goldsmiths College of Art, London, and was also commissioned to paint panels for the ceiling of the underwriting room in Lloyd's in 1931. During the Second World War he worked on ship camouflage. He has used foreshortening to produce an excellent impression of the hustle and gaiety of a lively holiday town, and the predominantly red and white colours used pick up those of the steamers' funnels. At the pier lie two LNER ships, probably *Kenilworth* and *Talisman*, while the CSP vessel has been banished to an end berth.

The pier buildings of 1882 can be seen to good advantage and the artist

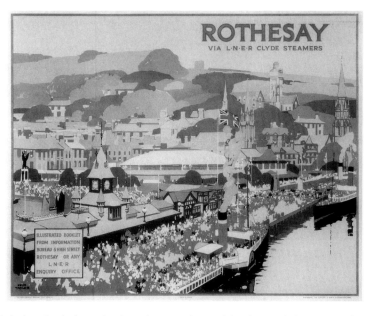

has tactfully omitted the clutter of huts and sheds with which they were surrounded over the years. There were plans to rebuild the pier in 1940, when it might have received a clock tower based on the Tower of Empire at the Empire Exhibition held in Glasgow in 1938, but these were frustrated by the war, post-war difficulties and official indecision; in the end it was only the burning of the existing buildings in 1962 that led to their replacement. The new building, a vaguely nautical box, in contemporary style, surmounted by a smaller box that looked like a motorship's funnel, had a shorter life than its predecessor, and was also claimed by fire, to be replaced in 1992 by the present more modest premises, in a rather pleasing rustic style.

The circular building beyond the pier is the Winter Garden, erected in 1923-24 on the site of the former bandstand. It was designed by the Burgh Surveyor, John Stephen, and provided for almost 50 years a home for what was generally known as 'the entertainers'. Glasgow holidaymakers could be very demanding and their reaction to a poor performance ensured that the entertainers *did* entertain! Pre-war, artists such as Tommy Lorne appeared, while in post-war times Grace Clark and Chic Murray headed the bill for many years. The building closed in the 1970s, but after years of decay and neglect it has now been refurbished and provides a restaurant with views of the bay as well as facilities for concerts and dancing.

At the extreme right of the picture is the spire of the West Church, and on the hill stands the grey Gothic Revival building of Rothesay Academy, erected in 1869 and sadly burned down in 1954. *National Railway Museum, York*

head. Thus the visitor could choose from a wide variety of accommodation, ranging from the Kyles of Bute and Glenburn Hydros through the Esplanade Hotel (tea, bed and breakfast, 8s 6d per night – electric light and gas fires) to a very modest room in a 'room and kitchen' (tenement flat) in Argyle Street. On Canada Hill there was also the 'Healtheries' holiday camp.

For day visitors, or those who did not take meals in their holiday accommodation, there was an abundance of restaurants, headed by Mrs Allan's, first established in 1846; it advertised all makes of chocolates and bon-bons and provided excellent lunches and high teas. Anyone who felt like a little something between meals could choose from

one of several ice-cream parlours, of which the most popular was Zavaroni's. Their cones (cornets) and sliders (wafers) were available from two shops in the town as well as from a kiosk at Ettrick Bay; although the latter no longer exists, the firm is still very much in business.

Although there are several places of interest in Bute, excursions were naturally limited by the island geography and the guide books enthused that 'no end of steamer excursions may be planned during a stay at Rothesay'. That was in 1930 when holidaymakers could, every day, choose from at least six all-day cruises and a host of afternoon trips. The more romantic perhaps preferred to wait for one of the evening cruises.

Below One of the great attractions of Rothesay was boating. From (at one time) five stands on the promenade to the west of the pier, hirers offered rowing and later also motor boats, to allow visitors to try their skill. One of these firms, James Gillespie, had been established as far back as 1860. At the end of the day, one of the motor boats would tow the rowing boats, like a trail of ducklings, past the steamers awaiting the last departures and round into the inner harbour for the night. It has to be said that the standard of oarsmanship was generally not high, and there were often near misses with

approaching steamers. Fortunately, however, there were very few accidents.

On a Saturday afternoon in September 1950, *Duchess of Montrose*, having helped out on the ferry services, heads back to Gourock, while rowing and motor boats (the latter with flags) await custom at one of the stands. On the left the bow of the submarine depot ship *Montclare*, a former Canadian Pacific liner, is just visible; she was built in 1921 and succeeded at Rothesay in 1954 by HMS *Adamant*, but in 1957 the location of the depot ship was moved to the Gareloch, somewhat to the detriment of the economy of Bute.

Opposite above Naturally the pier was the focus of much interest and attracted many who wanted simply to observe the bustle of the comings and goings of the steamers, as well as those who were actually going somewhere. Pier dues had been introduced in 1917 and remained at 2d until well into the 1950s. A public address system was installed in the 1930s and, between announcements of arrivals and departures, music, usually of a Scottish nature, was played, but otherwise there were no facilities for promenaders, and in fact nowhere to sit, unless one perched on a bollard. The gangways were always a favourite of children, as can be seen, since by running hard from one end to the other, an excellent see-saw effect could be produced! Generations of pier masters expended a great deal of energy in a usually futile attempt to stop this amusement!

The last passengers have just boarded *Mercury* of 1934 at Rothesay and the crew and pier staff prepare to remove the gangway, while keeping a watch for the inevitable last-minute arrival. G. E. Langmuir Collection, *courtesy of The Mitchell Library, Glasgow City Libraries*

Opposite below The most popular destination for trips outside the town was Ettrick Bay on the west coast. The main attraction there had always been the 'pure, limpid waters', but over the years these were supplemented by sand castle competitions and goat carriage and donkey rides. However, by the 1930s these were becoming rather old hat and the range of amenities had been extended to include a soda fountain, a milk bar, an 'Over the Top' funfair thrill and aeroplane flights. In 1932 a 15-inch gauge miniature railway was opened, and on this gyrated an American-style 4-4-0 locomotive, which in the 1960s was rescued from a scrapyard and is now preserved in Norfolk. No other relic of those days survives and only the 'pure, limpid waters' remain.

Until the end of the 1936 season, the trams of the Rothesay Tramways Company running from Rothesay to Ettrick Bay provided an attractive ride, from Port Bannatyne across open country, but in the following year they were replaced by buses and, even if these were modelled on the latest design used in Blackpool and carried the name 'Rothesay Tramways', another local institution had gone. This view, which dates from the

1920s, shows the front portion of one of the combination (part open, part closed) trams awaiting departure from Guildford Square. Beyond are a line of taxis; a shelter was later erected over this stand and is currently being renovated.

Beyond again lies the Williamson-Buchanan paddle steamer *Kylemore* of 1897 in what was officially Berth 1A, but unofficially the 'Kylemore berth', since she was virtually the only ship to use it! She normally spent the night at Rothesay, leaving at 8.15 am on what was largely a cargo run to Glasgow; when she returned, she often offered short evening cruises. On the extreme right are the pier gates, erected in 1917 when pier dues were introduced; to their left is the building that contains public conveniences of stunning Victorian splendour; fortunately these have been restored and are once again open to the public. *G. E. Langmuir Collection, courtesy of The Mitchell Library, Glasgow City Libraries*

Above For steamer operators, Ettrick Bay was sufficient of a resort in its own right to justify tours that bypassed Rothesay and landed passengers at Port Bannatyne pier, from where special cars took excursionists across the fields to the west coast. The new *Marchioness of Graham* is seen at that pier in September 1936, presumably on an evening cruise from

Arran. *G. E. Langmuir Collection, courtesy of The Mitchell Library, Glasgow City Libraries*

Below 'Several hundred laughing, eager holidaymakers come excitedly down the gangplank' was the caption to this illustration in the first post-war holiday guide to Bute of 1946. No doubt the writer wanted to convey a feeling of carefree pleasure, but it was in fact a bit at variance with reality, especially in 1945 when few steamers were running and crowds had to wait in long queues at Wemyss Bay and Rothesay to get aboard. Coming down the gangway was usually a time of crisis in the holiday, with shouted instructions to children to 'haud oan tae Auntie Lizzie' and anxiety about Granny and her suitcases becoming stuck fast half way down and bringing the whole operation to a standstill.

The steamer still carries her wartime abbreviation 'D of M'ROSE' on a detachable board hung over the rail, her hull is painted grey (liberally streaked with rust) and her saloon windows are boarded over, but the funnels have just been repainted yellow and black, as a portent of better times to come. *Author's collection*

Dunoon has much less of a history than Rothesay, the first recorded holidaymakers being the family of a Mr Reid, who rented a thatched farmhouse in 1775. Having survived a day-long journey by wherry from Glasgow – they spent some time aground on the way – they found that the only person with whom they could speak was the minister, as all the other inhabitants spoke only Gaelic. But they must have enjoyed themselves well enough because others followed and, perhaps rather later than Rothesay, the village blossomed into a holiday town, with about 9,000 inhabitants and, by 1930, more than four times that number of visitors in a holiday week.

Dunoon was well placed to have the best of both worlds. Although the journey by road from Glasgow was, and still is, too long to be any threat to the rail-steamer business, the hinterland of Cowal and Argyll offered many possibilities for coach tours, and even before 1914 the char-a-banc had made its appearance. By 1934 there were estimated to be 150 coaches, sometimes referred to as 'cars', operating in Cowal. Day trips were run to Oban and the Trossachs, the former being a round trip of 165

On a wet day around 1950, passengers hurry to board *Talisman* for Inellan and Rothesay; the plastic mac has now made its appearance. The view is taken from the upper deck and shows the signal cabin, with the central disc still showing clear for the steamer to come alongside. This type of apparatus was designed by Charles Allan (of the Allan Line, later merged with Canadian Pacific) in 1889 and was intended to eliminate the practice of racing for vacant berths at piers.

The signal boxes normally displayed three black discs on either side, but when the pier master had decided which of up to three approaching steamers could most safely berth, he worked a mechanism that pulled up the disc corresponding to the position of that steamer, which then displayed a white face by day and a white light by night; the mechanism was interlocked, so no other disc could then be moved. If only one steamer was approaching, only the central disc was used. By this time Dunoon was the only pier where the system regularly had to deal with several steamers, but the practice was continued until the 1970s, when the decline in steamer numbers made it superfluous. *The late John Thomas, courtesy of Dr Alasdair C. Harper*

miles and, perhaps, after almost 12 hours in a small Bedford or Chevrolet, a little tiring compared to a steamer cruise. But the tour operators called at many hotels to collect passengers and provided a door-to-door service impossible for the steamers. They also offered evening drives, very often in the form of mystery tours, which in practice might be no more than a run to an inn at Kilmun, where there would be a competition for the best child singer or the man with the knobbliest knees. But it sounded so very thrilling!

Nonetheless, for most people a holiday in Cowal meant steamer trips. The pier had been taken over by the Town Council in 1895 and was immediately rebuilt with attractive buildings in a vaguely Swiss chalet style, and extended to allow two steamers to berth at the same time. In 1937 an upper promenade was erected above the two

buildings to provide a vantage point for those who simply wanted to sit and watch the steamers without getting in the way of passengers, barrows, ropes and other hazards. An additional charge for this facility was made in pre-war days, but not after 1945. There was also a cafe and, as at Rothesay, a public address system with music. Dunoon was the Clyde's nearest approach to an English pleasure pier, and although the upper deck has now been removed, otherwise the pier is still substantially as rebuilt a hundred years ago. In 1936 almost 11,000 calls were made by steamers, the majority of course in the summer months.

Dunoon provided a good choice of facilities for visitors. Hotels ranged from McColls, which was totally rebuilt in 1938, a smooth Art Deco facade replacing the attractive but somewhat haphazard chalet-style building, through Rosegarth, with its

The steamers also offered evening trips, sometimes by the operators themselves but often under the auspices of a charter. Thus on 23 July 1938 *Duchess of Argyll* left at 6.10 pm for a 'Scotch Cruise' to Tighnabruaich, organised by HP Cruises; this had nothing to do with a brand of sauce often found in Dunoon boarding houses, the initials standing for Health and Pleasure Cruises. On board there were competitions where the ladies had to identify Mr McHaggis and the gents to find Miss McPurritch, to music provided by the Orlo Trio. There were prizes for the best 'Scotch' turns and, even if it did smack strongly of 'Highlandism', it was all good fun and excellent value for 2s 2d. The advertiser somehow forgot to mention the ferocious 'Scotch' midges that invade Tighnabruaich on a summer evening! This heavily retouched photograph shows *Queen Alexandra* setting off for such a cruise. *Author's collection*

QUEEN ALEXANDRA.

own putting-green, garage and separate tables for late, five-course dinner (3 guineas per week in the summer of 1934), to Mrs Hanley of 'Rosevale' who offered bed, breakfast and high tea for 42 shillings per week. Interestingly, as late as 1939 one hotel that had 56 bedrooms, and thus around 100 guests, had only four bathrooms, although there was of course separate lavatory accommodation.

Millport has always been and remains primarily a family resort, visited by generations of parents with young children. Until the coming of the car ferry, there were few motor vehicles other than a handful of taxis and what was known as the 'Millport Bus' – even in the 1940s a row of horse-drawn cabs greeted those arriving at the Old Pier, while a horse-brake, which started from the foot of Cardiff Street, offered an afternoon drive to Fintry Bay. Today, the cabs and brake have gone, and

although the bus fleet has increased by 200% and an open-top double-decker provides 'Round the Island' tours, there is still relatively little traffic.

Until 1972 the island of Cumbrae boasted two piers, the Old Pier and Keppel. The former, which is still in use, is in a rather exposed situation and certain passenger certificates displayed on board steamers carried the proviso 'Not to or from Milport in the event of a fresh southerly wind', which made a cruise to the island sound rather daring. When the pier was closed, and normally this happened only in winter, the 'Millport Bus' dashed back and forth between the town and Keppel until all intending passengers had been safely deposited there. The Old Pier was threatened with closure in recent years, but fortunately was substantially rebuilt with help form Argyll & Island Enterprise and was reopened to traffic with a special call from the car ferry *Saturn* on 4 April 1992.

Despite the amalgamation of the railway fleets in 1923, there were in the inter-war period still two distinct Millport services, one by (normally) *Marchioness of Breadalbane* from Wemyss Bay and one by the ex-GSWR *Glen Rosa* from her base at Fairlie. It is the latter seen here arriving at the Old Pier in 1925. Few people are meeting the steamer, suggesting that this is an off-season view; meeting the boat was a favourite pastime, even if no visitor was expected. *Glen Rosa* was a strongly built little ship and the only one of the former

GSWR fleet to be substantially rebuilt by the LMS; she was reboilered in 1926 and her bridge moved forward of the funnel, but the operation cost more (£20,000) and took longer than had been anticipated, so that the 1926 season was well advanced before she returned to service. If management had known of the difficulties and cost beforehand, she would probably not have been so favoured. In the event, she lasted in service until 1938 and went to the scrapyard the following year. *Author's collection*

THE PIER, MILLPORT.   33152

Above Carefree days on the Clyde. On 17 August 1939 *Queen-Empress* leaves Largs for Wemyss Bay, while behind her *Queen Mary II* heads off to Rothesay. In just six days the Nazi-Soviet pact will make war almost inevitable, but for the moment there is clearly much pleasure to be had messing about in boats. *G. E. Langmuir Collection, courtesy of The Mitchell Library, Glasgow City Libraries*

Below During wartime summers Millport had to depend almost exclusively on *Marchioness of Graham*, and residents and visitors became much attached to her. The town also had 'entertainers', who performed in a building that did not even boast the luxury of a floor - there was only bare earth underfoot - and Jimmy Donoghue and Jimmy Ramsay did their best to boost morale with songs deriding Hitler. One of these, to much applause, asserted that while 'He may sink a few more small boats . . . he'll never sink the *Marchioness of Graham*'. The ship is seen here in 1945. *G. E. Langmuir Collection, courtesy of The Mitchell Library, Glasgow City Libraries*

Cruising out of Ayr

The town of Ayr is the oldest port on the west coast of Scotland and by the time of Robert Burns had a thriving trade with Ireland and the highlands and islands. From 1821 steamers linked it with Glasgow and on 11 August 1827 one of the regular steamers, *Leven*, was advertised to cruise from the port round the 'Craig of Ailsa' to give passengers a near prospect of the 'stupendous natural curiosity'. The coming of the railway in 1841 ended the direct steamer service from Glasgow, but by the 1870s, helped by the Burns connection, Ayr had become both a destination for tourists and a resort for holidaymakers from the industrial towns. In the LMS holiday guide for 1939, the town advertised 'A Health Giving Holiday' and supported this claim by mentioning ample supplies of excellent water and perfect sanitation. Since by this time most people took both of these facilities for granted, these claims may not have done much for the town. However, visitors in search of something a little stronger than the 'excellent water' could avail themselves of Loyal Brand Australian wine, red or white, at 2s 6d per bottle from the shop of Mr John Ramsay of George Street.

In 1876 cruises from the harbour were begun by a steamer known officially as *Bonnie Doone* and unofficially, from her mechanical weakness, as *Bonnie Breakdoon*. Despite her problems, the sailings prospered and in 1898 the Glasgow & South Western Railway purchased for them the large sea-going paddle steamer *Juno*. Apart from the war years and 1919 she served Ayr faithfully until the close of the 1931 season. The following year she was replaced by the 'palatial' new turbine steamer *Duchess of Hamilton*, built, unusually for a Clyde steamer, by Harland & Wolff at their Govan shipyard and fitted with engines made in Belfast.

Apart from her fine accommodation, the new ship conferred another advantage on the holidaymakers of Ayr. Section 4 of the Glasgow & South Western Railway (Steam Vessels) Act of 1891 had expressly forbidden company ships to sail to Campbeltown or Inveraray or ports on the north and west coasts of Arran. Being registered with the Caledonian Steam Packet Company, *Duchess of Hamilton* was free of such restrictions and between 1930 and 1939 provided a range of cruises and standard of comfort not to be repeated in the annals of the port of Ayr, although she faced the competition of 'popular charabanc drives daily', not to mention visits by the LNER cruise ship *Jeanie Deans* until 1937 and occasional Sunday cross-Channel sailings to Ireland by Burns & Laird's *Lairds Isle*.

Excursions were resumed on 17 June 1947 by the smaller *Marchioness of Graham* of 1936, but some of the longer sails, such as that to Inveraray, had to be deleted from the programme due to her lack of speed. She held the fort until 1954 when replaced by the paddle steamer *Caledonia*. This steamer introduced forenoon 'cafe' cruises that were then being pioneered on the upper firth by 'Maid' Class motor vessels; the fare of 3s 6d included a cup of coffee and a chocolate biscuit (normally a Penguin), but as *Caledonia* did not actually go anywhere and simply paddled around the firth for 90 minutes, there were few takers and the cruises were dropped from the programme in later years. When *Caledonia* was needed at Craigendoran in 1965, day cruises ceased and holidaymakers had to make do with short trips offered by the steamer from Gourock once a week, and even these ended after 1970. But the passing of *Waverley* into the hands of the Paddle Steamer Preservation Society has brought a happy ending to the story, and today's tourists can with her enjoy sailings to a wide range of destinations, including the 'Stupendous Natural Curiosity'.

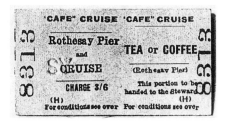

Above It is 1923 and *Juno* has just passed under the control of the London, Midland & Scottish Railway. To date the only sign of the change of ownership has been the painting of the lower part of the funnel yellow, but in the following year she would lose her grey hull and the handsome crest from the paddle box - rather pettily the LMS removed these crests from the ex-GSWR ships. The steamer is entering Ardrossan harbour, a port of call on most excursions, and the normal time of departure was 11.15 am. *Author's collection*

Below It seems almost incredible now that, after a full day's steaming to a destination such as Arrochar, *Juno* and later *Duchess of Hamilton* would immediately set off for an evening cruise from which ship and crew would not return to base until perhaps 10.30 pm. These cruises were given every Sunday and on several weekdays, Arran being the most common destination, although other resorts featured occasionally - on Friday 10 July 1936, for example, *Duchess of Hamilton* set off for that town from Ayr at 5.15 pm and Troon half an hour later, and gave passengers about 50 minutes ashore in Bute, returning to the Ayrshire resorts at 9.55 and 10.30. Coal and labour were both plentiful! The cruises were continued in the post-war years, but only as non-landing trips to the Arran coast.

The sunsets seen on such cruises could be magnificent, as in this view of *Juno* leaving Ayr in LMS days. The writer of the card was enthusiastic and wrote 'This is better than working'. *Author's collection*

Right *Duchess of Hamilton* at her berth in Ayr harbour in the late 1930s. At least three steam drifters are moored ahead of her, while on the nearer side of the harbour are two short sea cargo vessels, the nearer one being a steamship registered in Liverpool. That further away is one of the motorships *Lairdswood* or *Lairds Crest* of Burns & Laird Lines, both of which from 1936 operated a triangular Ardrossan-Belfast-Ayr service. *Author's collection*

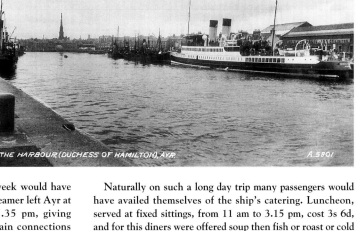

THE HARBOUR (DUCHESS OF HAMILTON) AYR.   A.5801

Below Along with her sister *Duchess of Montrose*, *Duchess of Hamilton* was operated as a one-class ship, at fares equivalent to 1st Class on other routes. On the trip to Lochgoilhead, for example, the return fare from Ayr or Troon was 5s 6d, at a time when £4 per week would have been considered a good weekly wage. The steamer left Ayr at 10 am and reached her destination at 1.35 pm, giving passengers an hour ashore. There were train connections from inland stations, and bus services linked Ayr station and Prestwick with the harbour, at a fare of 3d. Passengers from these stations were warned to book tickets in advance, to ensure accommodation aboard the steamer. The view shows *Duchess of Hamilton* at Lochgoilhead pier.

Naturally on such a long day trip many passengers would have availed themselves of the ship's catering. Luncheon, served at fixed sittings, from 11 am to 3.15 pm, cost 3s 6d, and for this diners were offered soup then fish or roast or cold meats, sweet, salad and cheese. The cruise programme stated that catering was suited to meet the requirements of all classes of the travelling public. Food was good but unimaginative, and the variety of dishes offered today on ships of Caledonian MacBrayne was unknown. *Author's collection*

THE PIER, LOCHGOILHEAD.

Left On many trips the Ayr steamer called at Troon. The harbour there had been acquired by the GSWR from private owners in 1902 and subsequently greatly improved; the massive steam cranes on the left probably date from that period. In August 1952 *Marchioness of Graham* has called en route to Lochgoilhead; leaving Troon at 10.40 am, she would not reach her destination until 2 pm, but passengers would still have an hour ashore. The return fare was now 9 shillings and lunch cost 4s 6d. At the mainmast flies the British Railways houseflag with the (emaciated) lion and wheel emblem; two years later Clyde steamers would revert to the CSP flag, which used the more sturdy lion rampant of Scotland.

Below On Sunday 22 July 1951 *Marchioness of Graham* leaves Dunoon on the return leg of a trip to the Gareloch. By that time the charms of the once pretty loch had been ruined by industrialisation, and it had become a dumping ground for unwanted warships; passengers on this trip had a good view of a battleship of the 'Duke of York' Class.

Above By the time *Caledonia* was providing the excursions, cruises tended to be shorter than in pre-war days, reflecting the improved working conditions of the crews, and were not given on every day of the week. One of the longer sails still offered was that to Tarbert via Lochranza, given twice in the 1954 season and leaving Ayr at 9.30 am. Passengers could spend 3 hours at the latter or over 1 hour at the former place. The fares from Ayr or Troon were 10s 6d and 8 shillings respectively. *Caledonia* is seen here swinging away from Lochranza and heading for the Kintyre coat. *Author's collection*

Right Apart from its excursions, Ayr was also a ship-repairing centre, and steamers were sometimes overhauled there in the yard of the Ayr Engineering & Constructional Company Ltd. In May 1951 *Duchess of Hamilton* and, beyond, *Marchioness of Graham* receive some pre-season attention. *King Edward* had already been dealt with.

Ayr was and is very much a working harbour. In 1919, in a last piece of expansionism, the port was taken into railway ownership by the Glasgow & South Western Railway, and therefore passed to the LMS in 1923. In 1938 the dredger *Carrick* was commissioned for service at Ayr. She was built by W. Simons & Co Ltd at Renfrew and launched complete with all machinery in March 1938 by Mrs J. D. Harris, wife of the Marine Superintendent. She could dredge up to 32 feet below water level. Fitted with two sets of triple-expansion engines and twin screws, it was said that she could do work that normally required two ships. *Carrick* was later transferred to the Docks & Inland Waterways Executive and her funnels were then lengthened and painted blue. In 1968 she was sold for service in Palermo, and was not broken up until 1984.

In this view she is heading out to sea from Ayr to dump the spoil from her dredging. She did not require the service of a separate hopper, having capacity to contain her own spoil, which was released through doors in the hull when she reached her destination. *World Ship Society, Cliff Parsons*

3. SOME STEAMERS

Glencoe

One of the most remarkable survivors in the MacBrayne fleet in the 1920s was the paddle steamer *Glencoe*, built in 1846 for the service from Glasgow to Stornoway, at that time run by Mr (later Sir) James Matheson, and named *Mary Jane* after his wife. She was originally flush-decked and was fitted with a steeple engine, then the last word in marine engineering. In 1851 she exchanged the storms of the Minch for the quieter waters of Loch Fyne, when she was sold to the Glasgow & Lochfyne Steam Packet Company,

which provided a very leisurely service from Glasgow to Inveraray. G&L ships carried cargo as well as passengers, and it was not unusual for up to 2 hours to be spent at intermediate piers en route. This company was taken over in 1857 by Hutcheson & Company, the predecessors of MacBrayne. In 1875 *Mary Jane* underwent fairly major surgery to lengthen her to 165 feet; she emerged with a saloon aft and a new bow, without the attractive bowsprit and figurehead previously carried, and to mark the transformation was renamed *Glencoe*.

She returned to the West Highlands and

Glencoe approaches Kyle of Lochalsh; the forward deck is well loaded with cargo. The steamer had no bridge; the steering wheel was located behind the funnel and the engine room telegraphs were on the paddle boxes. The captain, the second figure on the port box, stands with his hand on the telegraph, just behind the galley chimney. *Author's collection*

The origin and authorship of the following poem have been lost in history, but it was clearly written to commemorate the visit of *Glencoe* and *Lochfyne* to Glasgow in 1931. As far as it has been possible to trace the various references, these are explained in the footnotes, but many of the names cannot now be traced.

PS Glencoe sends Cheerio to 'New Lochfyne'

Lochfyne, Lochfyne, Dear Dainty One[1], you much
　　enhance our stock
Great tribute to that Sacred Isle[2] from old
　　Dumbarton's[3] Rock:
Let me thank you most sincerely, when there at
　　Glasgow Quay
I'm thinking yet the Folks were pleased 'Old Mary
　　Jane' to see.

When Ewan took me round from Kyle, to help with
　　'Civic Week'
Your fame had travelled North by then, but Fame I
　　ne'er did seek:
I've faced the Minch and Jura Sound, with Sea and
　　Wind Sou'West,
But I liked Portree and Mallaig Run, with Johnnie
　　Gillies[4] best.

The Boys first took the 'Clydesdale'[5] out, then led me
　　quietly in,
They took my 'Birth Certificate', no more I'll toil and
　　spin,
I paddled through Ardrossan Lock, the helm hard
　　a'port,
While Ewan worked the telegraph, a gentle kindly
　　sport:

When Calum got the ropes ashore, it dawned upon
　　me then,
I'm tied up with an Irishman, his bonnie name
　　'Lairdsben'[6].
Alone I missed the Gaelic, long years My Daily Hymn
Yet Jeffrey he was good to me and kind was Johnnie
　　Simm.

You've yet to see the last of me, so now the story goes,
My Golden Eagle rests in peace, with Great Sir
　　Arthur Rose[7].
My Brasses made up into lots, to different people sold,
Will yet appear in Bright Array, old Brass made into
　　Gold.

The figure of a golden eagle that surmounted the companionway to *Glencoe*'s dining saloon. This saloon was situated on the lower deck aft, and had been the original saloon when the ship was new; entry to it remained right at the stern, even after she had acquired a saloon on the main deck. Lachie, the Purser in the 1920s, held strong views about class distinction and was quick in pursuit of any steerage passenger who tried to invade this sanctum without first paying an excess fare. *Glasgow University Archives, McQueen Collection*

My Engines and that Lever Bar[8] are not just yet to
　　part,
They're 'Brolly' well looked after in the Galleries of
　　Art:
Had they just left my paddles too, how happy I would
　　be,
The Kelvin Water wander down, Old Meadowside to
　　see[9].

Ardrossan, 5 June 1931

1　*Lochfyne* was a sturdy, well-built ship, but hardly dainty!
2　The Sacred Isle is Iona, the destination of *Lochfyne*'s summer service until 1936.
3　She was built in the Dumbarton yard of Messrs Denny.
4　Johnnie Gillies was the last master of *Glencoe* and had been with the ship for many years.
5　*Clydesdale* was a MacBrayne cargo/passenger steamer, built in 1905 and withdrawn in 1953.
6　*Lairdsben* was a cargo and cattle carrier acquired by Burns & Laird Lines Ltd in April 1931 and withdrawn in 1936.
7　Lt Col Sir Hugh Arthur Rose (Bart) was Chairman of the Caledonian Steam Packet Company from 1930 to 1937 and a Director of David MacBrayne Ltd for the same period. He had presumably acquired the golden eagle from the after deck.
8　A lever bar was sometimes required to start the engines.
9　The River Kelvin passes the Art Gallery and enters the Clyde near Meadowside, the birthplace of *Glencoe*.

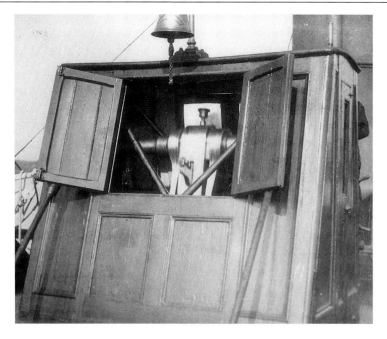

The steeple engine was invented in 1832 by David Napier and took its name from its supposed resemblance, in profile, to a church steeple. It operated vertically, rather than horizontally, thus requiring less space within the hull of a ship; it also had the merit of avoiding the surging fore and aft motion of the early diagonal engines, which on a long journey could become very tiring to passengers. The drawback was that it needed additional headroom, and on *Glencoe* the crosshead had to be sheltered in a small deckhouse of its own! The problem of space meant that this type of engine could not be developed beyond the original concept and it was obsolete by 1865. By the 1920s very few engineers could have had experience of working a steeple engine, but this was no problem to Mr Latto, who, as Chief Engineer, knew how to get the best out of *Glencoe*. *Glasgow University Archives, McQueen Collection*

worked various services, finally settling down on the Islay station until replaced by the new *Pioneer* in 1906. Thereafter she went north to operate the Mallaig-Kyle-Portree mail service, on which, with some breaks during the war when she ran on the Clyde once again, she remained until withdrawn in 1931.

There have of course been other paddle steamers that have survived longer, but these have in all cases been summer-only excursion ships, operating on fairly sheltered waters such as the River Elbe at Dresden. Right up to May 1931 *Glencoe* was trading all year on some of the most exposed waters around Britain and was doing so with total reliability. Her clinker-built hull must have been made of strong stuff and her longevity was a great tribute to her builders, Tod & McGregor of Meadowside, Glasgow. They also engined the ship, and her machinery likewise lasted until the end, although she was reboiled three times. In 1901 she had acquired a rather fatter funnel and this in part helped to disguise her age, although of course latterly her passenger accommodation fell far short of what both regulars and tourists were coming to expect. In fact, there really was no covered accommodation for steerage passengers other than the alleyways by the engine room.

When she ran her last trip, in May 1931, she was brought up to Glasgow and, during Glasgow Civic Week, was exhibited at Broomielaw alongside the new *Lochfyne*. There could hardly have been a greater contrast between two ships, the old paddle steamer with the (by 1931) totally antiquated steeple engine and the new diesel-electric ship with excellent accommodation for both classes and, in the observation lounge, a soda fountain. After the exhibition was over, *Glencoe* made her own way to Ardrossan, where she was broken up. However, the engine was preserved by the Glasgow Art Gallery and Museum, although it is at present not on display.

Claymore - 'Great sword of the Hebrides'

This extremely pretty ship was built in 1881 for the passenger and cargo service between Glasgow and Stornoway, at a time when it formed the principal link between the capital of Lewis and the outside world. Even when built she was of rather old-fashioned appearance, since by that date coastal ships were of more utilitarian build, but her clipper bow, bowsprit and figurehead of a Highlander combined to set off the fine lines of a shapely hull, and she was a joy to look upon. The accommodation too was definitely traditional, and the berths opened out from the saloon, which was located in the after part of the hull. But none of this detracted from her appeal, which seemed to grow as the years advanced and ships of her beauty became rarer.

Claymore normally left Glasgow around lunchtime on Thursday and picked up passengers at Greenock, Custom House Quay, at 6 pm. She reached Oban at 8 am the following morning and Kyle at 10 pm the same evening. Arrival at Stornoway was scheduled for 6 pm on Saturday. The route, so stated the MacBrayne timetable, was through scenery rich in historical interest and unequalled for grandeur and variety. She did not at any time deviate from the service for which she was built and was not called up for war service, although she was camouflaged when the submarine menace was at its height.

By 1920 the direct route to Lewis had lost out to the rail/sea journey as a means of actually getting there, and Claymore was laid up in winter, a cargo-only service being provided by Clydesdale. However, in summer she was as busy as ever, but with holidaymakers who looked on the round trip as a cruise and enjoyed the old-world atmosphere on board, sharing one long table with the officers. At this time she was commanded by Captain James MacKechnie and the mate was Robert MacLean, later in command of Saint Columba on the Clyde. Her trips were booked up well in advance, some regulars booking at the end of one voyage for the next year! Such was the affection in which she was held that there was a great outcry when, in 1929, her hull was briefly painted grey, but this was nothing to the regret that accompanied her withdrawal in 1931. Her last departure from Glasgow was on 13 May and she then sailed direct from Stornoway to Bo'ness on the Forth, where she was broken up. Requests for souvenirs came in from every corner of the globe.

Several of her admirers commemorated her in verse, at least one, appropriately, in Gaelic. This verse is written as though from Glencoe, although the actual author is unknown:

> Claymore thou King of all the West, I greet you ere we're parted,
> You always were a Gallant Gay and never were downhearted;
> I've seen you rolling the Mull, then lying quiet at Kyle,
> Old 'Mary Jane' aye looked on you, that Boy with happy smile.

She was replaced by Lochbroom, acquired from the Aberdeen Steam Navigation Company and actually ten years older than Claymore. She had, however, been modernised and could offer accommodation, such as single-berth cabins, more in keeping with the demands of passengers of the 1930s. There was also a music room and hot salt water baths. Her route was changed, so that from Kyle she sailed to Portree in Skye then doubled back to the mainland and called at Gairloch, Ullapool and Lochinver; some sailings were extended to Lochinchard. In 1936 fares for this cruise ranged from £11 11s for a single cabin to £6 10s for a berth in the gentlemen's cabin. Lochbroom sailed from Glasgow approximately every ten days and the season lasted from 14 May to 19 October.

In 1937 Lochbroom was replaced by the larger Lochgarry, but that ship was a war loss and the cruises were not resumed after 1945, although a few passengers were carried on the Stornoway cargo ship until that service ceased in 1974. Today similar cruises can be enjoyed aboard Hebridean Princess, formerly the car ferry Columba.

Armadale Pier, Skye

Above While *Claymore* discharges cargo at Armadale pier, some lady passengers take advantage of the break to stretch their legs with a walk into the village. Armadale is one of the piers that, thanks to the car ferry, now sees a volume of traffic undreamed of in the days of *Claymore*. *Author's collection*

Below Mallaig is one of the places famed for West Highland sunsets. Against one of these *Lochbroom* sets out for Kyle. *Author's collection*

SUNSET AT MALLAIG. 218608.J.V.

Duchess of Fife

Few ships have combined good looks and sound performance in the measure shown by this paddle steamer. She was lunched at the Fairfield yard in 1903 for the Caledonian Steam Packet Company and has been called 'the ideal hull model and design for a Clyde passenger steamer'. She was in fact designed by Professor P. A. Hillhouse, who later held the chair of Naval Architecture at the University of Glasgow. All her life, apart from war service, was spent on the railway connection services from Gourock and Wemyss Bay. She was thought worth reconditioning after her return in 1945, although ships that were her juniors were scrapped, and she put in another eight years of service, mainly on the Millport station, until she made her last run on 6 June 1953. She was sadly missed.

Above There were naturally some adventures for a ship that, for her entire career, operated all the year round, and the worst in *Fife*'s career took place on an August morning in 1936. When working an early Rothesay-Gourock direct service she ran aground in thick fog at Kirn, when she did not quite make it to the pier on a strong ebb tide. She remained stuck for a day, the damage to her dignity being as great as the damage to her hull. In this view one of the tugs of the Clyde Shipping Company stands by ready to attempt to tow her off, while the LNER's *Marmion* sails past. *Author's collection*

Left The elaborately decorated paddle box of *Duchess of Fife*, seen when she was laid up in the Albert Harbour, Greenock, in the summer of 1953. The arms carried are those of Princess Louise, daughter of Edward VII, who married the Duke of Fife. The couple had opened the Glasgow Exhibition of 1901 and were very popular in Scotland. The boxes were strengthened with cross-bracing during a post-war refit, which rather spoiled their appearance.

Duchess of Fife's saloon had, in pre-war days, an unusual circular settee, which was in fact arranged around a ventilator to the dining saloon below. This attractive feature was not replaced when she was reconditioned after war service. The ship was fitted with electric light from the beginning, although the lamps tended to give off a rather modest glow, but elaborate oil lamps were also carried as a back-up. *McLean Museum and Art Gallery, Inverclyde District Council*

The second *Glen Sannox*

One of the first matters to engage the attention of the Scottish steamboat sub-committee of the new LMS was the replacement of the boilers of *Glen Sannox* of 1892, and tenders for this work were accepted from five yards in 1924. However, closer inspection of the steamer revealed that it would not simply be a straightforward replacement job, that supports and flooring would have to be renewed, and that the total cost could be almost £40,000.

To spend so much on a 32-year-old uneconomical ship was out of the question, and Beardmore let it be known that it could build a new ship for £57,000. Denny was then asked to tender and duly received an order for a new turbine steamer, at a contract price of £58,000, which in the event was slightly exceeded. Either to keep the price down or to ensure delivery by May 1925, the firm simply dusted down the plans of *Duchess of Argyll* of 1906 and thus produced a steamer that, if fast, was already obsolete when new. A correspondent in a Cowal newspaper suggested that she was to be called *Duchess of Atholl* and would in fact be a replacement for the *Argyll*, which was to be sent to England, but there would appear to have been no foundation for this suggestion.

The appearance of *King George V* in the next year showed just how conservative the LMS had been, and later Denny prepared a plan for the enclosure of the midships part of the promenade deck of *Glen Sannox*, rather as was done with *Queen Alexandra*. This provided for the enclosure of the deck from below the forward funnel to the end of the upper deck, with a single, double-width embarkation door just under the second funnel and the windows carried to the end. A pencil amendment was then made to show an opening at the end, as on *Duchess of Montrose*, but shorter. However, probably due to opposition from Captain Beasley, Marine Superintendent of the LMS, the plan was dropped and *Glen Sannox* retained her classic lines to the end.

Above Fairly early in her career *Glen Sannox* draws into the pier at Lamlash, while some bowlers enjoy a game on the adjacent green. Bowling was a favourite pastime of holidaymakers, and local clubs welcomed visitors; a common charge at that time seems to have been 6d per game. *G. E. Langmuir Collection, courtesy of The Mitchell Library, Glasgow City Libraries*

Below The Clyde is not always a picture of serenity, and Arran steamers especially had to be prepared to face rough seas, even in summer. In this view, taken from Saltcoats in September 1934, *Glen Sannox* heads out from Ardrossan into a south-westerly gale. *G. E. Langmuir Collection, courtesy of The Mitchell Library, Glasgow City Libraries*

King George V

Just as *King Edward* had been a revolutionary ship in 1901, her successor, *King George V*, was one of the most innovative ships of the 1920s. The development of the motorship had by this time seriously begun to challenge the steam engine for economy, and the machinery fitted to the new ship for Turbine Steamers Ltd was intended to evaluate the possibilities of the high-pressure turbine, fed by steam from water-tube boilers, in providing a similar degree of economy. The turbines were manufactured by Parsons and the boilers by Yarrow & Company. Naturally with high-pressure turbines in operation, there had to be a supply of steam at similar pressure, and on *King George V* this was delivered at a pressure of 550 lbs per sq in.

Passengers, however, were much more interested in the facilities of the new ship. The promenade deck was enclosed amidships, to allow a good view of the scenery from a sheltered position, and the 1st Class dining saloon, which could seat 120 diners, was on the main deck aft.

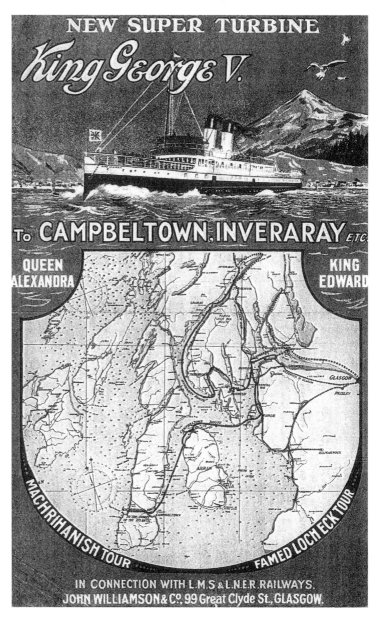

A poster produced by Turbine Steamers Ltd before the ship actually entered service. The original illustration is in vivid pre-Raphaelite blue, yellow and green, and appears to show her dashing across Brodick Bay, with Goatfell in the background, although in service she did not normally sail there. The lifeboats on the upper deck were situated amidships, not forward as in the drawing.

The company was naturally very proud of its latest acquisition and in its brochure hailed her as 'the (Clyde's) greatest contribution to the science of marine engineering since . . . the first commercial turbine-propelled vessel, the *King Edward*'. The comfort of the 'large, airy dining saloon, the cosy tea lounge, the smoke room and ladies' cabin . . . bespeak the solicitude of the Management for their patrons' enjoyment'. The publicity then went on to give some details of the new type of machinery, and concluded that 'Great things are expected of the *King George V* - some say she (or should it be "he"?) will revolutionise modern shipping'. *Author's collection*

The aft mooring platform was on the promenade deck, rather than on a quarter deck, and this gave the ship a most handsome, smooth profile. She was sometimes referred to as the 'super turbine'.

King George V was launched at Denny's yard, Dumbarton, on 29 April 1926. Her sponsor was Lady Parsons, who was presented with a sapphire brooch to mark the occasion. Unfortunately the General Strike broke out just after her launch and this, coupled with some problems with the machinery, delayed her entry into traffic from the planned date of the end of June to 8 September, when she sailed to Campbeltown, although she was most commonly used on the Inveraray cruise.

In general, *King George V* gave much satisfaction, but there were a number of breakdowns, including one when passengers had to spend a night aboard, and she acquired a reputation for unreliability. More alarmingly, there were two incidents of the bursting of steam tubes, in one of which two firemen died of scalding; fortunately the ship was not carrying passengers at the time. However, the second accident happened on a July Friday when she was crowded with passengers and there was considerable alarm when clouds of smoke invaded

the accommodation. The ship dropped anchor off Pirnmill and her passengers were rescued by the veteran *Davaar*. Finally, in 1935 the high-pressure turbine and boilers were removed and a normal boiler fitted. Technically the experiment was considered successful overall, but the economies obtained would have been significant only in a ship that was running day in, day out all the year round; for an excursion steamer the complications were not justified.

In this converted condition she was sold late in the same year to MacBrayne and, apart form the war years, proved to be a most valued member of that fleet until retirement in 1974. Perhaps more than any other individual ship, she was to tourists *the* Scottish steamer, and thousands of visitors of all nationalities trod her decks over the years.

Sold early in 1975, she languished in dock at Cardiff for several years and it seemed that her only future lay in the scrapyard. Then in 1981 she was sold to Bass Charrington, who were looking for a ship to replace *Old Caledonia*, and work began on a total renovation. Sadly, just a few days before this was completed, fire broke out and the ship was gutted. In 1984 her hulk was beached at the mouth of the River Taff and left to the elements for demolition.

During her first three years of service, *King George V* had two slim funnels and the upper deck lifeboats were located beside these. In this condition she arrives at Tighnabruaich when returning from Inveraray to Greenock. *Author's collection*

Above When first reboilered in 1929, with boilers by Babcock & Wilcox, her funnels received cowl tops and the boats were moved to the end of the upper deck. This view of her off Craigmore would appear to have been taken from a rowing boat. *Author's collection*

Below In her later years *King George V* became a very popular ship for charter by enthusiasts' clubs. Of these occasions the most enterprising was that of 16 May 1970, when she cruised from Ayr to Bangor, County Down, for the Coastal Cruising Association. She is seen here approaching the pier at the latter port. *Dr Alasdair C. Harper*

Duchess of Montrose

From 1927 the management of the CSP must have been acutely aware of the threat posed by *King George V* to its own cruise ships, the newest of which was *Duchess of Argyll*; although she was a very popular ship with the travelling public, no one could pretend that her facilities were up to date. Sir Alexander Gracie, Chairman of the CSP from 1925 to 1930, and Charles Ker, a Director, suggested in December 1928 that the CSP should consider building a steamer with sheltered accommodation on deck. For some time this was opposed by Captain Beasley, Marine Superintendent of the LMS, who gave as his reason the need for the steamers to be able to carry cars. Eventually his objections were overcome and it was agreed to order for the 1930 season a new turbine for use solely on cruises.

The plan was approved by the LMS Board, but was then vetoed by the Chairman, Sir Josiah Stamp, this being the only occasion on which he overturned a decision of the Scottish Local Committee. Whether he did so on the grounds of cost alone or whether the idea of a ship built just for pleasure cruising was anathema to him – he was of a somewhat ascetic disposition – is now not clear. Nor is it known exactly when and by whom his arm was then twisted, but there was clearly some lobbying behind the scenes and two months later, in November 1929, permission to proceed with the new vessel was given, and an order went to Denny of Dumbarton.

Work then went ahead very quickly and *Duchess of Montrose* was launched on 10 May 1930 by Mrs Beasley. It was sad that Sir Alexander Gracie, who had taken a very close personal interest in the new ship – it was he who suggested having 'Lloyd loom' basket chairs in the observation lounge – did not live to see her completed.

When she entered service on Tuesday 1 July the public at once realised that a new era in Clyde cruising had begun. For the first time the ship was laid out on a one-class basis, avoiding the need to duplicate all facilities and imparting to the vessel an air of spacious luxury unknown in rival steamers. In all other respects, apart from the machinery, the CSP paid Turbine Steamers Ltd the compliment of copying *King George V*. The dining saloon was on the main deck aft, approached through a vestibule panelled in polished mahogany. The (originally) all-electric galley was aft of this saloon, to keep cooking smells away from passengers, and the sight of the galley boy sitting out on the aft quarter deck peeling quantities of potatoes was for long a feature of the cruises. Below the dining saloon were two auxiliary saloons or tea rooms and a bar, which was unfortunately fitted out as an 'Olde English' inn, with plaster walls, oak beams and brass lanterns. Still, it was cosy enough.

Otherwise the ship had an air of restrained modernity, nowhere more evident than in the lounge forward on the main deck. Here comfortable easy chairs, some grouped around small tables, were arranged informally, as in a hotel foyer, and pretty chintz curtains hung at the (rather small) windows. It all made quite a change from the long sofas and rectangular seating bays of *Glen Sannox*!

The engine room was slightly more open than on earlier turbines, to allow passengers a view of the dials, thus in part compensating for the loss of atmosphere compared with paddle steamers. The machinery itself was traditional direct-drive turbines driving triple screws. Apart from an embarrassing breakdown before the ship had even reached Dunoon on her maiden voyage, these performed reliably and ran with great smoothness.

Such luxury did not come cheap, and one wonders if Sir Josiah winced as he signed a cheque for the final instalment of the purchase price of £74,832, £32 over the contract price. This price was almost £5,000 more than that of *King George V*, where a disproportionate amount went on the novel machinery; on the new *Duchess*, the money went on the furnishings. The expenditure proved to be worth while, however, as the public loved her and flocked to patronise her cruises. For the 'Palatial New Turbine Steamer' an attractive programme was devised, taking her on a 'Round of the lochs and Firth of Clyde' on Mondays and Fridays, round Arran and Ailsa Craig on Tuesdays and to Ayr on Wednesdays. Perhaps the greatest novelty was the revival of the day cruise to Stranraer on Thursdays; in practice, this allowed only an hour ashore and, given the length of the pier, only those who walked very smartly would have seen anything of the town, but the coastal scenery en route was magnificent. Afternoon cruises were given on Saturdays and Sundays, but as a one-class ship she could not be used on ferry runs on Saturday mornings, so had these off service. Apart from the substitution of a cruise to Inveraray for the Stranraer trip after 1936, the programme continued until 1939.

As Duchess of Montrose was back at Gourock by 5.55 pm on most days, she was often immediately dispatched on an evening cruise, either as a public sailing or a charter. The latter were sometimes to an unusual destination, such as 'Gee Gee Island' (Horse Island, off Ardrossan). Novelty events were staged on board on many trips and life for the Purser and his junior assistants must have been difficult on one such cruise in August 1932, when they were asked to adjudicate on a competition to find 'the most irregularly dressed lady'!

During the war, 'D of M'ROSE', as she had now become according to the detachable board hung on her rail (see page 61), was the Wemyss Bay-Rothesay ferry steamer and carried a vast number of passengers as well as much general cargo. The saloon windows were blacked out, milk churns were piled high on the after deck and the decks themselves were torn and scarred by the iron wheels of the cargo barrows. It was a demanding task for a ship built for pleasure cruising, and somehow she took a long time to recover from it.

Post-war, Duchess of Montrose settled down to a modified version of her pre-war trips, but the Arran/Ailsa Craig cruise was not revived and she often alternated on the Campbeltown run with her sister Duchess of Hamilton. In 1952 she had a brief spell on the 'all the way' services, and she often relieved Queen Mary II on these at other times. As class distinction had now been abolished on CSP ships, she was used for ferry runs at the weekend, usually between Rothesay and Wemyss Bay. But her old sparkle had gone; she was the last ship to re-appear in peacetime livery, in 1947, and until she was converted for oil firing in 1957 she often ran late. Thereafter she revived and was at her post-war best in her last two seasons.

The inevitable end came with a cruise to Catacol Bay on 30 August 1964, and just over a year later she was towed away to be scrapped at Ghent. Few ships have given so much pleasure to so many people.

Duchess of Montrose enters Rothesay Bay during her first summer. The writers of this postcard were sailing on her every day and were enthusiastic about the interior decor, the turbine machinery and the orchestra. *Author's collection*

While other ships merely had a band, *Duchess of Montrose* had an orchestra, the Kaye Orchestra. This had been started by Jimmy Kaye and Harry Hunter, and had become very popular ashore; it was no surprise, therefore, that they were given the contract to play on this crack ship, favouring light classical music. The Kaye Orchestra remained on board for each summer of the 1930s and became known to thousands, while in winter they were frequently engaged for dances ashore. In this view Jimmy Kaye, the leader, holds his violin, and other members identified are Harry Hunter, pianist, and Billy, the saxophonist. *Mrs K. Hunter*

Right In the immediate post-war period, *Duchess of Montrose* continued to be used on ferry runs and, while so engaged on 4 October 1947, ran aground at Kirn with over 100 passengers aboard. The first ship on the scene was *Marchioness of Lorne*, and she made a gallant attempt to tow the *Duchess* off; unfortunately all that happened was that the rope broke. A second attempt by *Duchess of Hamilton* and *King Edward* ended the same way. However, the ship floated clear early the next morning and the damage was soon repaired. When she ran aground, passengers were transferred to the other steamers or to Kirn pier, using a launch belonging to a Mr Ferguson of Kilmun, and this is just visible to the left of *Duchess of Montrose*. A. S. Brown

Below A view looking aft along the alleyway beside the engine room in the 1950s; the rather spartan seating in this area was used only at peak periods. *Author's collection*

Lochearn and *Lochmor*

Part of the financial 'rescue package' of 1928 for MacBrayne stipulated that within four years the company, now David MacBrayne (1928) Ltd, would build four new ships for its services. The first was *Lochness* of the Stornoway service, the second and third were the subject of this section, and *Lochfyne* was the fourth. They were the only pair of sister ships built for MacBrayne.

Both ships were built by the Ardrossan Dockyard Company and were launched in April and May 1930 respectively. In accommodation they were an enormous advance on the ships they replaced (*Cygnet* and *Plover*), especially with regard to 3rd Class. For passengers travelling 1st Class there were cabins with the luxury of hot and cold running water and reading lamps above the bunks. In the dining saloon small tables replaced the long ones of the older ships.

Unfortunately the diesel engines were a disappointment, since they were very noisy and proved to be incapable of driving the ships at the 12½ knots that had been promised; instead they could manage about 9½ in reasonable conditions.

When *Plover* was replaced by *Lochmor*, her captain, Duncan Robertson, and many of the crew transferred to the new ship, which must, to them, have been a totally different kind of animal from the elderly steamship. They soon learned her tricks, however, and their efforts ensured that she settled in to perform a service as reliable as *Plover* had provided. Captain Robertson had a great reputation locally as a weather forecaster. This photograph of him was taken on *Lochmor* at Lochboisdale about 1934. *Margaret Shaw Campbell, Isle of Canna*

When faced with a strong wind and/or well loaded with cargo, they put their noses down and their sterns up and progress was even more leisurely. In 1948 and 1949 the ships were re-engined with new Paxman-Ricardo diesels and some improvement in speed was obtained, along with a reduction in noise levels.

Lochearn began her career on the mail service from Oban to Barra and Lochboisdale, while her sister was stationed at Mallaig for what was known as the Outer Islands run, which was basically a circuit of Skye extended to Lochboisdale with calls at piers in Harris and North Uist. On certain runs both ships met at Lochboisdale, allowing captains and crew to socialise and exchange news. From 1948 Lochearn became spare ship until 1956, when she was transferred to the Oban-Tobermory run in place of Lochinvar. As such she was the first ship to call at the new pier at Craignure in December 1963. She inaugurated the car ferry service to Mull in May 1964 and was later replaced by the new Columba.

Lochmor, on the other hand, remained on her original service for almost all her life, apart from time off to be re-engined in 1948/49. She made her last run on it in April 1964 and, on being replaced by Hebrides, was dispatched to Mallaig to begin the car ferry service to Armadale. When in turn Clansman appeared for that service, she went south to Oban to help her sister on the Mull ferry until Columba appeared. Despite their age and hard work, both ships were sold for further service in Greece, Lochearn being renamed Amimomi, and Lochmor becoming Naias, and they were not scrapped until the mid-1970s, although latterly they spent much time laid up.

Lochearn approaching Craignure on 20 May 1964 when acting as a car ferry.

Jeanie Deans

It is perhaps surprising that the paddle steamer launched by Miss Rhoda Whitelaw, at the Fairfield yard on 7 April 1931 for the London & North Eastern Railway, should have become such a favourite of both the travelling public and steamer enthusiasts. While her triple-expansion machinery was thoroughly up to date, her passenger accommodation was in many respects old-fashioned, when compared with other new ships of the period such as her great rival *Duchess of Montrose* or *Royal Eagle* on the Thames. On the promenade deck there was at first absolutely no shelter from the weather. The 1st Class lounge, aft on the main deck, was a handsome apartment, panelled in light oak and decorated with etchings from Scott's 'Heart of Midlothian'. It was described as being 'large and airy', but it was laid out in the same manner as that on *Columba*, built 53 years earlier, and showed no concession to modern taste.

The dining saloon (when the ship was new) was on the lower deck, fitted with 'artistic sideboards' and also laid out in traditional style, with small portholes that allowed diners no view of the passing scene. A dressing room for what were termed 'first class gentlemen' was also provided, in addition to the normal toilet accommodation, and there were book and confectionery stalls near the entrance to the saloon. For snacks in between meal times, or, as the LNER press handout put it, 'for passengers partaking of light meals', there was a small tea room, with tables for four. The inboard wall of this room had leaded mirrors to maximise the natural light available, and there was a sideboard with display cabinet, in which no doubt a mouth-watering array of scones, teabread and cakes was displayed. Facilities for steerage passengers comprised a saloon on the main deck forward, fitted with teak sparred seats, and a combined dining saloon and bar on the lower deck, with benchwood seats. This was a steamer of the 1890s, not the 1930s. What then was the secret of her appeal?

Perhaps it was her speed. From the start she was fast – although on trial she had not quite come up to her contract speed – and possessed a rakish elegance totally lacking in her turbine competitors. Her machinery was exceptionally smooth-running. But perhaps it was also the challenge that the cash-starved LNER dared to mount to the might of Gourock that appealed to the sporting instinct of the Clyde public; just as her namesake had set out from Edinburgh to London to conquer Queen Caroline, so she was setting out from Craigendoran to take on several *Duchesses*, not to mention a *Queen* and a couple of *Kings*.

In fact, in 1934 she quite literally took on *King George V* off Garroch Head when, in one of the Clyde's more spectacular accidents, the two ships collided on a clear day in a flat calm. *Jeanie* was on a charter to Arran, while the turbine was on the regular sailing to Campbeltown; they approached at 90 degrees to each other and neither gave way until it was too late, and *Jeanie*'s bow had plunged into the other's midships quarter, sending passengers sprawling on the deck with the force of the impact. Witnesses assigned blame equally to both captains. Fortunately no one was hurt, but it was an accident that should not have happened. The paddler returned to Rothesay and disembarked her passengers; she was off for four days for repairs. But this had been an exception, and normally, under command of Captain Duncan Campbell, she led a charmed life.

For its new ship the LNER provided an attractive programme of excursions from 1932 to 1937, much along the lines of those offered by *Duchess of Montrose* from Gourock to Ayr, Arran and Ailsa Craig, but *Jeanie Deans* called at Girvan on alternate Mondays in 1936 and 1937. Calls were also frequently made at Kilchattan Bay on Bute, a pier not otherwise visited by cruise ships. The cruise fares for 3rd Class and Saloon from Glasgow were identical to that on the CSP ship (7 shillings), but of course 3rd Class fares were also offered at 5s 8d from Glasgow stations, and this must have brought some additional traffic. In addition, meal prices in 3rd Class were below those in 1st, and a cold luncheon could be had for 2 shillings, while the cheapest midday meal on *Duchess of Montrose* was 3s 6d. Evening cruises were also given, including the novelty of 'radio cruises'. But the attempts to compete with the CSP on long-distance cruising finally proved to be too much for the LNER finances, and in the last years of peace *Jeanie Deans* worked the Loch Long and Loch Goil excursion.

Her war service was distinguished, and in one of the lighter moments she took on and beat *Royal Eagle*, the pride of the Thames excursion trade. When she reappeared on the Clyde in 1946 she was much altered, as will be seen from the illustrations – the young girl of the 1930s had become distinctly matronly! But her accommodation had been much improved, especially by the removal of the dining saloon to the main deck, from where diners could view the scenery as they ate, and she retained all her old popularity. If her speed had been somewhat impaired, she could still outpace her new consort *Waverley*. From 1950 she settled down to a routine of the new afternoon cruise round Bute – one of the few signs of enterprise shown by British Railways on the Clyde at that time – often in connection with coach tours at Craigendoran, and this was varied only in her

last four years on the Clyde, when she began to exchange rosters with *Waverley* and revisited her old haunts in the Lochs, as well as venturing to other parts of the Firth. Conversion to oil firing in 1957 also brought back her old capacity for speed.

However, with the decline in passenger numbers in the 1960s, it was inevitable that the older steamers would be withdrawn, and 1964 was the last season for *Jeanie Deans*. Her Clyde career ended on 28 September, ironically on the Wemyss Bay-Rothesay ferry. The next day she retired to join her erstwhile rival the *Montrose* in the Albert Harbour at Greenock, where she lay until overhaul in October 1965 prior to her departure for the Thames.

Thus passed from the Clyde one of the most popular ships of all time – a ship that brought a great deal of pleasure to very many people.

A deck view, looking forward from the after deck shelter, while the steamer lay at Arrochar in the 1930s. G. E. Langmuir Collection, courtesy of The Mitchell Library, Glasgow City Libraries

Above In her first year, the funnels of *Jeanie Deans* were distinctly short and there were complaints about the amount of soot and sparks that rained down on passengers sunning themselves on the after deck. The columns of smoke being produced as she leaves Dunoon suggest that the complaints were well founded! The absence of any kind of shelter on the promenade deck will also be noted. *G. E. Langmuir Collection, courtesy of The Mitchell Library, Glasgow City Libraries*

Left To remedy the soot problem, the funnels were heightened, the forward one by 9 feet, the after by 6. This gave her an unusual, jaunty appearance, and evidently caused some comment; LNER publicity then explained that this arrangement ensured that any smoke from the first funnel would pass clear of the second, and the possibility of soot falling on the deck be avoided. It did not say anything about smoke from the second funnel, but in any event the remedy seems to have worked. An observation lounge, furnished with 'Lloyd loom' chairs, was also fitted forward of the bridge. The alterations, carried out by the builders, cost £770 and the result can be clearly seen in this view of the steamer approaching Dunoon between 1932 and 1935. *G. E. Langmuir Collection, courtesy of The Mitchell Library, Glasgow City Libraries*

The majestic appearance of *Jeanie Deans* in post-war condition is well illustrated in this view of her arrival at Rothesay in early British Railways days. Although she now has yellow and black funnels, her deckhouses are still in LNER brown. *The late John Thomas, courtesy of Dr Alasdair C. Harper*

P.S. "JEANIE DEANS," Bowling

Departure of Cunard-White Star Liner
"QUEEN MARY"
from Clydebank on 24th March, 1936

LUNCHEON

Consomme Turtle
Cream of Cauliflower

Salmon Mayonnaise
Cucumber

Roast Beef　　　　　　　　Ox Tongue
　Roast Lamb　　　Mint Sauce
　　Chicken and York Ham
　　Potatoes　　　　Vegetables
　　　　　Salads

　"Queen Mary" Souffle
"Jeanie Deans" Charlotte

Cheddar　　　　　　　　　Cream
　　　Tea　　　Coffee

Above The original 1st Class dining saloon, with the traditional long tables. *G. E. Langmuir Collection, courtesy of The Mitchell Library, Glasgow City Libraries*

Above right One of the oddest 'sailings' ever performed by any Clyde steamer was that given by *Jeanie Deans* in

March 1936, when the liner *Queen Mary* went down the river. The ship was used as a floating grandstand in Bowling harbour and did not actually move from her winter lay-up berth! Nevertheless, the 'service' proved popular, as no doubt did the lunch that followed. *Author's collection*

Streamlined paddle steamers: *Mercury* and *Caledonia*

By 1934 the craze for 'streamlining' was well and truly established. The first railway locomotive so designed appeared, motor cars shed their angular, upright image and the liner *Queen Mary*, with her rounded superstructure and elliptical funnels, was about to be launched. What more natural then than for the LMS/CSP management to consider a pair of streamlined paddle steamers to replace its ageing tonnage in the Clyde fleet? In late 1933 it became known that two new ships had been ordered, one from Denny of Dumbarton and one from Fairfield of Govan. The latter, named *Mercury*, was ready first and actually appeared before the end of the winter timetable. There were unidentified problems with *Caledonia* even before she left the yard, and she was therefore later into service than her half-sister.

No paddle steamers quite like these had ever been seen in British waters. In some ways, the design was similar to that of *Royal Eagle*, built for

service on the Thames in 1931, in that there was an upper deck for passengers, but there the resemblance ended, for *Royal Eagle*, despite her fine facilities, looked clumsy, as though various parts had been added as an afterthought. The new Clyde ships were well designed and fully in the idiom of the period. The hulls terminated in a rounded cruiser stern, the superstructure forward was executed in a sweeping streamlined curve, surmounted by a solid white bulwark, and the after deckhouse, though partly concealed by the upper deck, was similarly rounded. To the horror of traditionalists, the paddle boxes were just that – white boxes above deck level, with slits in the hull that could be mistaken for windows. Indeed, when the ships were later camouflaged, it was very hard to tell exactly where the paddles were! *Mercury* carried a funnel of fairly conventional design, but that of *Caledonia* was almost exaggeratedly streamlined, being large and elliptical in section. The innovations extended to the machinery, and three-crank, triple-expansion engines were fitted for the first time in this fleet.

Passengers noted with approval the spacious deck shelters and roomy dining saloons for both classes. That for 1st Class passengers had small tables for four arranged in the centre, another novelty. Especially striking was the bar on *Caledonia*, which was fitted out with tub armchairs upholstered in red leather and decorated with a mural, carved in oak, on which were depicted various forms of transport, such as a trolleybus and an airliner vaguely like the Handley Page HP42. The ships were capacious and, even when loaded to near their capacity of 2,000, did not seem crowded, as there was ample circulating space. When they were on winter service there was some criticism about the absence of the old type of general saloon, and in later years one dining saloon was then used in this capacity.

Both ships were used on ferry work, with some short afternoon cruises, but each had problems. *Mercury* proved awkward to handle, and her sister was prone to mechanical breakdown; improvements were later made to both to cure these troubles. During the war both were called up as minesweepers, but the career of *Mercury* was sadly cut short on Christmas day 1940, when a mine exploded under her stern and, despite a gallant attempt at rescue, she sank after a tow of 4 hours. As HMS *Goatfell*, however, *Caledonia* seemed to lead a charmed life, later as an anti-aircraft defence ship. She was in Normandy on D Day plus 5 and later assisted in the relief of Antwerp.

After her return to peacetime duties, she was used on ferry runs, but after 1954 became a cruise ship, at first at Ayr, then, from 1965, at Craigendoran. Her early troubles were over and she ran well and was very popular. In 1970 she was sold to Bass Charrington and began a new career as a restaurant ship on the Thames. Wisely her new owners made as few alterations as possible and she retained all her old character. It was a great pity that a fire in 1980 damaged her so badly that she was fit only for the scrapyard. Her engines have fortunately been saved.

At a time when paddle steamers still ran in all-year-round service,
Caledonia **clears Rothesay Bay on the sunny morning of 3 October 1953.**

Left In earlier years, and well loaded, *Mercury* sweeps out into Rothesay Bay. She was technically owned by the LMS for the first three years of her career and is flying that company's houseflag. *Author's collection*

Below left One of the duties that came *Mercury's* way from time to time was that of tendering to liners anchored at the Tail o' the Bank, off Greenock. This was invariably done from Princes Pier, with special trains in connection from St Enoch station in Glasgow. On this blustery day in the 1930s, *Mercury* is about to take out a full complement to a Cunard liner, most probably *Andania* or *Ausonia*, these being employed on the service from Liverpool and Greenock to Canada. By this time the days of mass emigration were over and many of those travelling would by holidaymakers taking advantage of the new Tourist Class fares being offered on the North Atlantic. *Author's collection*

Three North British stalwarts

The North British Steam Packet Company and, from 1902, the railway company of the same name, followed a tradition of building ships that were simple, reliable and economical to run. While they may have lacked some of the refinement of the CSP ships, they served the Clyde well enough for many years and probably cost their owners a good deal less than the fliers of Gourock. This section illustrates three of these well-loved ships.

In 1936 the LNER introduced a simplified livery of grey hull and white upperworks to replace its attractive but no doubt costly colour scheme of black hull, cream saloons and varnished teak deckhouses. The first steamer to carry the new livery was *Kenilworth*, and the painters are seen putting the finishing touches to her at Craigendoran in March 1936.

Kenilworth

This work-horse was built by A. & J. Inglis at Pointhouse, Glasgow, for the NBSP Company in 1898, passing to the LNER in 1923. Almost all her career was spent on the service from Craigendoran to Rothesay and the Kyles of Bute. She was quite fast, though not a greyhound, and led a blameless existence, during which she must have given pleasure to hundreds of thousands of travellers. With retrenchment of LNER services after the 1937 season she became superfluous, and in January 1938 was sold, very unusually, to her builders for scrapping. She was spared the indignity of being towed to her last berth and paddled up the river to end her career where she had begun it.

She was the only ship to have a black line on the hull; this improved the rather bland appearance, but was omitted at the next repaint. The other steamers, *Marmion* on the right and *Waverley*, whose paddle box is just visible on the left, still wear the old colours. *G. E. Langmuir Collection, courtesy of The Mitchell Library, Glasgow City Libraries*

Kenilworth makes a vigorous start for Rothesay, as she casts off from Craigendoran in 1937. In a moment seated passengers will begin to sway back and forth in time to the rhythm of her single-crank engine, the last in service on the Clyde. Eight return journeys to Rothesay were made, Monday to Friday, in the height of that summer, and the Saloon return fare from Craigendoran was 2s 7½d, but for those who liked a bargain there was an afternoon return fare of 1s 6d. *G. E. Langmuir Collection, courtesy of The Mitchell Library, Glasgow City Libraries*

Marmion

This is an example of a ship that began well and ended well, after her career had had an unfortunate hiatus. She was built in 1906 for the Arrochar service of the North British Railway and was luxuriously fitted out. She was well liked by tourists making the Three Lochs Tour and also gave evening cruises from coast resorts. When called up for war service, her promenade deck was extended to the bow, and this feature was retained when she resumed civilian service in 1920. But her speed, never great, had dropped to the point where she could not maintain any service, and she also had a distressing tendency to roll. She was therefore laid up while a long argument ensued between the NBR (from 1923 the LNER) and the Admiralty, but in the end that august body did agree to pay for alterations. In 1923 the promenade deck was cut well back, and finally in 1926 *Marmion* resumed normal service, being usually employed between Craigendoran, Rothesay and the Kyles of Bute.

In 1932 she was extensively overhauled and her saloon completely renovated on modern lines. The old rectangular bays of sofas were taken out and comfortable easy chairs and occasional tables installed in their place, and part of the space was fitted out as a tea room; these alterations proved popular with passengers. *Marmion* was again called up for war service in 1939, and was bombed and sunk at Harwich in 1941.

Above Despite her poor performance, *Marmion* looked elegant enough in 1920, and the gentleman oarsman in the boat has eased off to allow his lady passengers to admire her as she leaves Dunoon in that year. *Author's collection*

Below Disembarking from *Marmion* at Craigendoran in the late 1920s. It is clearly a very low tide - it was not unknown for ships to rest on the bottom at that pier - and as passengers crowd to the port side the ship has taken on quite a list, causing the angle of the gangway to become even more acute

and no doubt posing problems for some elderly folk. Beyond the ship in the distance the handsome station buildings and covered footbridge can be seen. In the bay platform to the right, one of the ex-NBR 4-4-2 'Yorkie' tank engines and a line of NBR-style bogie carriages form the boat train, which would run up to Glasgow (Queen Street) in about 40 minutes. Today the pier is in ruins and the station demoted to a halt on the Helensburgh electric line; trains take about the same time, although calling at more stations en route. *Author's collection*

Marmion and her reflection on the firth in the early 1930s. G. E. Langmuir Collection, courtesy of The Mitchell Library, Glasgow City Libraries

Lucy Ashton

So much has already been written about this ship that it is difficult to find anything more to say! Her story might almost border on a fairy tale, of the very ordinary little paddle steamer that, when new, was scarcely noticed beside the then stars of the Clyde – *Columba, Glen Sannox* or *Lord of the Isles* – and later was quite outclassed by the swift turbines, but which went on to cheat the shipbreaker on at least two occasions and about which a booklet was written and a radio programme produced when she celebrated her diamond jubilee. Not only that, but by her efforts to maintain the Craigendoran sailings single-handed during the Second World War she achieved a reputation for sheer hard work and persistence shared by few other steamers. In 1942, for example, she carried 200,000 passengers and much additional cargo, and during the entire war period missed only ten days from service, in 1944.

During this period of intensive working, her accommodation was improved by the conversion of part of the saloon into a cosy little tea room, situated right aft. And then, when it seemed that finally it was all over, she re-emerged as the world's first jet-propelled ship to zoom around the firth in the interests of research into the resistance of ships' hulls.

The facts of her career can be briefly summarised. She was built at the Rutherglen yard of T. B. Seath in 1888 for the North British Steam Packet Company, and was used on the Holy Loch and later Gareloch services. In 1902, having suffered an embarrassing failure of her machinery just as she was coming in to Princes Pier, she was re-engined with compound engines. She might have been replaced (indirectly) by the new *Fair Maid* of 1915, had that ship survived to carry passengers, and she might have been scrapped in 1938, had the diesel *Talisman* been more reliable and war not looming. But she survived. Her last passenger voyage was made in February 1949 and she finally passed to her last resting place in 1951. It had been a fine career.

Perhaps the cruellest events of her life were her exclusion from the Gareloch after 1942 and the repainting of her funnel in BR yellow and black in 1948; the former was dictated by military necessity, the latter by bureaucratic indifference.

Until the mid-1950s almost all Clyde steamers were coal-burners, and coaling was a laborious, dirty and time-consuming business. At Gourock it was done directly from railway wagons, a convoy of men running barrows across a plank and on to the ship, where the coals went down a chute into the bunkers. At Craigendoran there was no provision to take railway trucks down the pier, and the coal had to be transhipped by cart. This scene dates from 29 November 1918, just two weeks after the Armistice, and shows *Lucy Ashton* being coaled at **Craigendoran.** *G. E. Langmuir Collection, courtesy of The Mitchell Library, Glasgow City Libraries*

Below Between the wars *Lucy Ashton* became closely associated with the service to the piers on the Gareloch. Five round trips were made each weekday in 1930, one only going as far as Clynder, and, like all LNER services, they were timed to the minute; the entire journey took 50 minutes from Craigendoran. By this time only piers on the west side of the loch were served, those on the east bank having lost out to the bus. As the CSP with the Holy Loch service, the LNER advertised the service as an afternoon cruise and the timetable called it 'a most enjoyable outing'. Through fares of 2s 9d and 2 shillings (Saloon) were advertised from Rothesay and Dunoon respectively, and from Helensburgh the charge was a modest 1s 2d (joining *Lucy Ashton* at Helensburgh could be problematical, as the timetable warned that she might not call at low tide). Between her Gareloch runs she provided a ferry service across to Greenock five times daily, with an extra sailing on Saturday, and she was thus in constant commission for just over 12 hours, from

7.25 am to 7.50 pm. On Saturday her day did not end until 9.5 pm, at Princes Pier. Coaling and taking on water and stores occupied the spare 40 minutes between 9.50 and 10.30 am at Craigendoran. It was a demanding schedule for a 50-year-old veteran!

This view from the early 1930s shows *Lucy Ashton* approaching Helensburgh, with, in the background, the old wooden warship *Empress* that for many years was stationed at the mouth of the Gareloch as an 'industrial training ship'. *Author's collection*

Bottom Lucy Ashton celebrated the end of the war in Europe in 1945 by being the first of the Clyde steamers to have her funnel repainted in peacetime colours, although the hull remained grey until 1946. From July 1945 she gamely added two daily trips to Rothesay to her schedule, as an answer to the revival of the Gourock-Rothesay service by CSP. Her progress was stately rather than speedy, but the sight of that

red/white/black funnel coming round by Craigmore lifted the hearts of many Rothesay people. At this time, it was reported, she had a 'lady purser' who was in fact the assistant; even so, this marked a real breakthrough for the Clyde steamers, on which women had been confined to the catering side.

During the war *Lucy Ashton* had been commanded jointly by Captains D. Campbell and A. McPhail, both of whom retired in September 1945. A pleasing little ceremony was held on board on that occasion when regular passengers presented cheques to both officers and a piper marked the occasion with some appropriate music. This view shows the steamer as she appeared in 1945. *Author's collection*

Little ships and 'puffers'

Quite apart from the glamorous excursion steamers or the hard-working car ferries, the Clyde has always required some little ships to provide short trips or to reach places that were not normally visited by the larger vessels. They seldom made the limelight, yet many people still remember with pleasure a trip from Rothesay to Loch Ridden on *Gay Queen* – the owner of which resolutely refused to change the name of his vessel when 'gay' acquired a new meaning in the 1970s – or a sail back to Millport on *Wee Cumbrae* in the evening after the larger steamers were tied up for the night.

Right After the small 'Clutha' waterbuses ceased running in 1903, the only way to see Glasgow harbour and the shipyards was to sail on one of the steamers running to the coast from Glasgow, but this required more time than many visitors to the city could afford. In 1938, when a record number of such visitors was expected to come to the Empire Exhibition held in that year in Bellahouston Park, the CSP management decided to order from Denny of Dumbarton two small motor ships that would provide short trips from Bridge Wharf to Clydebank, where passengers could also admire the new Cunarder 'No 552' at John Brown's yard. Named *Ashton* and *Leven* and given yacht-like white hulls, the two little ships went into service in June 1938. In view of the wet weather of that summer, it might have been better if the saloons had been fitted with larger windows, since little could be seen through the portholes, but they carried 82,000 people in the season and were clearly successful enough for the cruises to be repeated in 1939, in

which year the two ships had black hulls. This is the 1939 schedule. *Author's collection*

Below *Leven* passing Yoker in 1938. G. E. Langmuir Collection, *courtesy of The Mitchell Library, Glasgow City Libraries*

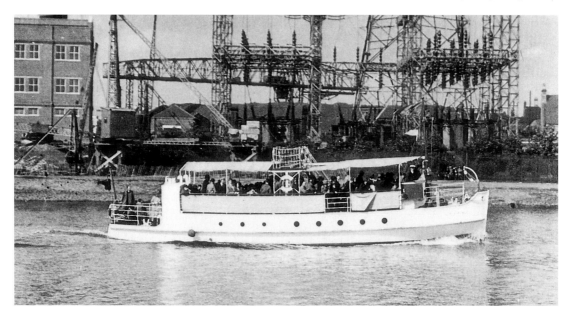

Above After war service as tenders at Gourock, both ships were transferred to ferry runs from Gourock to Dunoon and, later, from Largs to Millport, and they are seen here together at the former pier on a Saturday in July 1953. Eleven return trips were made daily, and on Saturdays, to cope with heavy traffic, they worked alternate sailings together, the others being taken by *Countess of Breadalbane*. Crew members watch apprehensively as *Leven* comes alongside *Ashton*, and others pull the gangway into position. Largs pier was a busy place on a Saturday and the bow of *Maid of Skelmorlie* can be glimpsed behind the motor vessels.

As can be seen, access to the ships was not easy and, when there was an attempt to use them on winter duties in 1952 there was a considerable outcry in the Glasgow press, citing in particular the difficulties for elderly passengers. The *Evening News* reported the sad story of a lady who normally travelled by steamer from Kilcreggan to Gourock, then by us to Greenock, but who would in future have to take a bus to Helensburgh, train to Glasgow and train back down from Glasgow, rather than trust herself to *Ashton* or *Leven*. After a week the public had made the point and the pair were taken off until summer. Despite this, both ships had fairly long careers with CSP, being finally sold in 1965; both then went on to give over 20 years service to new owners, *Ashton* ultimately becoming *Wyre Lady*, and *Leven*, renamed as *Pride of the Bay*, being recorded at Jersey as late as 1986.

Left Apart from *Gay Queen* already mentioned, which was in fact successor to a *May Queen*, Rothesay also had another motor vessel, *Maid of Bute*, built in 1937. From a berth in the inner harbour she gave cruises to Loch Striven, Tighnabruaich and, occasionally, Dunoon, where she is seen in June 1959. Sometimes she was chartered to the CSP for the evening run to the Kyles. Although somewhat vividly painted - her hull was at different times bright green and mustard yellow - she was quite a comfortable vessel and many holidaymakers took advantage of her cruises. She was owned by Mr John Knox until sold in 1973 to a Fort William owner, then later to owners at South Queensferry, who renamed her *Maid of the Forth* and used her on trips similar to those given some time earlier by *The Second Snark*. She was later replaced by a new ship.

Right In 1955 David MacBrayne purchased a fishing boat, *Irene Julia*, which was converted for passenger/cargo service and renamed *Loch Toscaig*. She had been built in 1945 as one of a class of Motor Fishing Vessels, used as tenders at naval bases. At first she was used by MacBrayne for a service from Kyle of Lochalsh to Toscaig, and thus relieved the Stornoway mail ship of the necessity of calling at Applecross. Later she was transferred to Oban for the Lismore service, and is seen here at the North Pier in May 1964, by which date her hull had been repainted blue. *Claymore* of 1955 is in the background at the Railway Pier, and the fine overall roof of the station can be seen; this has since been removed and today the platforms are completely devoid of shelter. *Loch*

Toscaig was not transferred to Caledonian MacBrayne in 1973, remaining the property of David MacBrayne Ltd until sold in 1976, having been replaced by a car ferry.

Right Few little ships have aroused both antagonism and affection in the measure of *Countess of Breadalbane*. She was built in 1936 to develop the tourist traffic on Loch Awe and replaced the steamer of the same name. In pre-war days she made a daily run to Ford from Loch Awe pier, and evening cruises were also given. Her accommodation, though compact, was of a high standard, including a dining saloon, and she became most popular. Services were resumed in 1948, the time allowed at Ford now being reduced to allow the ship to preform a 2-hour non-landing cruise from Loch Awe pier on three days per week. Apart from tours by rail and steamer from both Oban and Glasgow, a circular tour was also provided by W. Alexander coach to and from Ford via the Pass of Melfort, at a fare of 18s 5d 3rd Class rail from Oban.

However, in order to rationalise the Clyde services it was decided to transfer *Countess of Breadalbane* to the firth, this being done in April 1952. Attempts to use her on winter services provoked an outcry and led to the appearance of a poster (anonymous) announcing 'FOR SALE - the desirable vessel *Countess of Breadalbane*, complete with oars'! But once she had settled down and, later, been re-engined, she became a most useful and popular member of the fleet and performed all sorts of duties, from the Largs-Millport ferry to cruises and a late Saturday run from Gourock to Rothesay. From 1967 until its closure in 1971 she was on the Holy Loch service.

She was by no means finished when CSP had no further use for her, and was sold to a local owner in Gourock, by whom she was renamed *Countess of Kempock* and used on the upper firth ferry runs. Her owner having died, she was in 1979 and 1980 chartered for service from Iona to Staffa, and coped well with the exposed waters of the Atlantic coast. She then had another complete change, and another overland journey, and in 1982 entered service on Loch Lomond as *Countess Fiona* for the Alloa Brewery Company. She had, at

last, also acquired a funnel! Her promenade deck was later totally enclosed amidships and altogether she presented a smart and modern appearance, quite belying her half century. However, she suffered the various changes of ownership also experienced by *Maid of the Loch*, and has not sailed since 1989, remaining laid up at Balloch, her future uncertain.

Few ships have had such a varied career - from summer butterfly on a sheltered inland loch to year-round ferry on the Clyde - and she has coped well in all her roles. Many remember her with affection and it is to be hoped that she will not be left to rust away.

The photograph shows her approaching Dunoon pier in 1959, with *Maid of Cumbrae* on the left. In that year she gave an afternoon cruise from Largs to Dunoon continuing, on most days, to the Holy Loch. The *Maid* is on a Rothesay-Craigendoran service.

During the Second World War the relatively safe Clyde anchorage was the main port used for traffic to and from North America, and Gourock and Greenock had to deal with an unprecedented volume of troop and cargo movements. This involved the LMS in running 5,477 special trains to and from Gourock and 4,308 to and from Greenock Princes Pier (which since 1940 had not been used for civilian traffic). The steamers had also of course to carry the normal year-round traffic, and between 1939 and 1945 CSP ships carried 17 million passengers, not far short of their normal carryings and certainly more than would have been carried on the regular services, apart from cruises. To service the ships using the Clyde Emergency Port, 16 tenders were ultimately required and these were placed under CSP management.

One of the ships involved was the tender *Smeaton*, seen here off Gourock in the summer of 1945, with *Queen Mary II* in the background; the funnels of the Clyde steamer have been repainted yellow, but the hull is still grey. *Smeaton*, named after the designer of the first Eddystone lighthouse, was by now a very old lady, having been built in 1883 for tender work at Plymouth for the Great Western Railway. In 1929 she was replaced by a modern ship and was sold to W. T. McCalla of Belfast, for excursion work on Belfast Lough and tender duties as required. She passed to the Ulster Steam Tender Company in 1937 and was requisitioned on the outbreak of war for similar work at Gourock. She was scrapped in 1947. *G. E. Langmuir Collection, courtesy of The Mitchell Library, Glasgow City Libraries*

Almost as well known as the passenger steamers were the Clyde 'puffers' – the little cargo boats that ran to almost all places on the Clyde and the Western Islands and that have now, save for a few examples surviving in preservation, completely disappeared. Some were specialised, but most made their living by carrying general cargoes, and they became a familiar sight, either tied up alongside a pier (very often a stone quay no longer used by passenger ships), or butting their way down the firth and through the channels between the islands. Other than their crews, few ever trod their decks, yet some were as well known as the most famous of the passenger steamers. The televising in the mid-1960s and again in recent times of stories from Neil Munro's 'Para Handy' tales have brought the 'puffers' to a wider audience than they knew in their prime.

No one, except perhaps Para Handy himself, could have considered them beautiful, but they had a certain purposeful charm and their colour schemes, in which red largely figured, blended in well with the scenery. They were tubby little ships, their length, with the exception of the last few to be built, being determined by the dimensions of the locks on the Forth & Clyde Canal. Within their dimensions they were surprisingly capacious and, to those who watched the unloading of a 'puffer', it was surprising how much could come out of the hold. They were bluff-bowed and excellent sea boats, although when loaded their freeboard was not very much above water level and they could be wet in a heavy sea. The hull was rounded underneath, to allow the 'puffer' to run ashore at places that did not boast the luxury of a pier. Until near the end all were steam-powered, although from around 1914 they no longer 'puffed' in the strict sense of the word. For most of their time, 'puffers' had a totally open bridge, wheelhouses being fitted to a few only in the 1950s. The last steam-propelled boat in normal service was withdrawn in 1967.

Above *Rivercloy* unloads into a stout Dodge lorry at Inveraray pier on 17 June 1952. She was one of a fleet owned by G. & G. Hamilton of Brodick and, apart from the wheelhouse, is very much a traditional 'puffer'. In 1952 *Jeanie Deans*, on the other side of the pier, was not assigned to any regular service and divided her time between relieving other steamers (as here) and running cruises, such as that around Arran, which had not been given since 1939. *World Ship Society, George Osbon*

Below No view of Millport harbour would be complete without the 'puffer' *Saxon*. She had been built as *Dane* in 1903 and, after a collision in 1925, was acquired by Walter Kerr of Millport. For the next 40 years she kept Cumbrae supplied with coal and sometimes other goods. She then blossomed into a film star, being used in the first 'Para Handy' series for the BBC in 1965/66. She would have made an ideal candidate for preservation, but shortly afterwards was broken up. In this view, from May 1963, she shares the pier with the CSP motor vessel *Leven* and a motor yacht. Containers on flat trucks await the next visit of the car ferry, and the mainmast of *Talisman* is just visible on the right of the picture.

Above The 'puffer' *Gael* unloads at the old stone quay at Lamlash on 26 May 1960.

Below The 'puffers' did of course serve places well beyond the Clyde, and this view shows *Rivercloy* discharging coal at Onich, Loch Leven, in August 1930. She was another of the Hamilton fleet. *National Maritime Museum, London*

4. ON HIGHLAND LOCHS

Many of Scotland's inland lochs have in the past enjoyed a steamer service, these being started both to provide transport for lochside communities and to allow tourists to view the scenery from the water. At one time some lochs, such as Loch Lomond, even formed part of a through route from the centre of Scotland to the West Highlands. The coming of the railways ended that function, and that of the motor bus and lorry the need to serve the local populace. In recent times even the tourist aspect of such sailings has declined, and today only Loch Katrine can boast the services of a steamer, although motor launches do provide trips on other lochs.

Given the number of ships – both handsome paddle seamer veterans and well-appointed modern motorships – that ply Swiss lakes, it is little short of a national disgrace that the situation in Scotland should be thus, and in particular that the beautiful *Maid of the Loch* should have been allowed to go out of service to save a few thousand pounds, to be left to disintegrate over the years. From the Swiss experience it is clear that preservation and the continued running of such ships is too important to be left to private enterprise alone, and that a partnership of all concerned – national and local government, private companies and enthusiasts – is required to ensure that the ships survive to delight thousands of tourists every year.

Thanks to the efforts of a group of preservationists and the very active support of Dumbarton District Council, *Maid of the Loch* has not fallen apart at her Balloch moorings, as once seemed inevitable, and has regained something of her former appearance, although it is at present uncertain if visitors will ever again be able to enjoy a cruise on Loch Lomond aboard her.

In earlier years a winter service was provided on Loch Lomond, all year round until 1914, then on three days per week until 1933. To work such services and to give short cruises from Balloch around the islands, the Caledonian and North British Railways, whose Dumbarton & Balloch Joint Committee maintained the sailings from 1896, purchased in 1914 two of the former London County Council river steamers, with which a service had been maintained from 1905 to 1907. It was no more successful than later attempts to run waterbuses on the Thames have proved, and the ships were sold to private owners. In due course both *Shakespeare* and *Earl Godwin* were bought by the joint administration, the former being renamed *Princess Patricia* and the latter *Queen Mary*; unfortunately the latter was gutted by fire soon after she arrived in Scotland and there is no evidence that she ever sailed on the loch. *Princess Patricia*, however, became a useful member of the fleet and

sailed until the end of the 1937 season. She was later broken up at Balloch. This view shows her alongside the pier there and dates from 1919. *Glasgow University Archives, McQueen Collection*

Below Services on Loch Tay, in central Scotland, were started in 1882 by the Loch Tay Steamboat Company Ltd, formed by the Marquis of Breadalbane, to provide goods and passenger services to the lochside villages. The Marquis was closely connected with the Caledonian Railway and was the first Chairman of the CSP. There were six piers on the loch and at one time four double runs were given each day, one of these being an express for tourists. Circular tours by rail, coach and steamer were arranged from places such as Aberfeldy and Perth. Even by 1917 road transport was beginning to make the services uneconomic, and in 1921 the struggling concern had to suspend all sailings. It was bought by the Caledonian Railway for a fairly nominal figure and the running of the steamers was entrusted to the CSP. Services resumed in 1922. There were two passenger steamers, *Lady of the Lake* and *Queen of the Lake*, one passenger/cargo

vessel, *Sybilla*, and a cargo boat, *Carlotta*, which had been laid up since 1910 and was not recommissioned.

This photograph of *Sybilla* must have been taken in 1922, since she is wearing the yellow funnel of the CSP. She had been reboilered in 1920 at a cost of £763 4s 7d, but despite this was withdrawn from service in 1927, the winter sailings having ceased in 1925 and the cargo runs in the following year. She is here towing one of the barges that were used to carry heavy loads of coal or timber. *G. E. Langmuir Collection, courtesy of The Mitchell Library, Glasgow City Libraries*

Bottom The passenger steamers that ran on Loch Awe were more closely connected with the tourist trade, there being, until 1935, cargo steamers that catered for local needs. One of the passenger ships was the first *Countess of Breadalbane*, built in 1882 for the then owner of the Loch Awe Hotel. She did not sail from 1914 to 1922 when she was taken over by the Caledonian Railway, passing to the LMS in the following year. Various circular tours were run in connection with her sailings, from both Oban and Glasgow, and in the 1920s motor coaches took over from horse-brakes on the road portions of these tours, between Ford and Oban. The dainty little *Countess* is seen here at Ford pier in the late 1920s. The CSP had in 1926 taken over the Oban, Ford & Loch Awe Syndicate and replaced that concern's obsolete vehicles by modern coaches such as the Albion Viking shown here; the bodywork was by Beatonson of Glasgow. *Countess of Breadalbane* continued to sail until 1935 and was replaced by a new motorship the following year. *G. E. Langmuir Collection, courtesy of The Mitchell Library, Glasgow City Libraries*

'The Tour par Excellence' – 'This excursion must be done, come of the other what will'. So ran a heading in the LNER timetable above a map of the route of the Three Lochs Tour. And indeed it was one of the most scenically attractive of all the Clyde cruises, providing also for tourists a chance to sail on Loch Lomond, from a base at one of the Clyde resorts.

It was also one of the oldest established, dating back to at least 1850, when the railway line to Balloch at the head of Loch Lomond was opened. The Clyde part of the tour, to Arrochar at the head of Loch Long, was nominally looked after by the Lochgoil & Lochlong Steamboat Company, but in 1865, fearing that this link was being neglected, the Lochlomond Steam Boat Company had built for the service the second *Chancellor*, following her by another steamer of the same name in 1880. This ship worked closely with the North British Railway, and when she was sold to the Glasgow & South Western Railway the NB itself entered the trade in 1891 with the luxurious new *Lady Rowena*, followed by *Marmion* in 1906.

After 1919 the Clyde link was worked by *Waverley*, with *Jeanie Deans* appearing in 1931 from 1937; after the Second World War the service was provided by the new *Waverley*, latterly helped by a 'Maid' Class vessel. The last season of this famous tour was 1972.

In its heyday, the tour steamer started from Rothesay, passengers from Craigendoran transferring to her at Dunoon. Calling then at Blairmore, she reached Lochgoilhead around noon and Arrochar an hour later. Passengers could then walk or take a bus across to Tarbet on Loch Lomond, and sail down to Balloch where trains of both the LMS and LNER awaited them for Glasgow. (This was the only point at which the LMS had any direct participation in the tour, otherwise an LNER preserve.) Those going back to the coast changed at Dumbarton. The tour could be made in the reverse direction, in which the Clyde steamer went back to Craigendoran before going on to Dunoon and Rothesay. In 1938 the fare from Glasgow, 3rd Class and Saloon, was 6s 6d, which by 1965 had risen to 21s 3d.

The timetable warned that passengers had to find their own way between Arrochar and Tarbet, but that privately operated buses could be used; one is seen in the early 1920s at Arrochar, with *Waverley* at the pier. *Author's collection*

THE PIER, ARROCHAR.

Above On Loch Lomond the steamers normally providing the connection were one of *Princess May*, *Prince George* or *Prince Edward*. The first two had been built in 1898 and even then were old-fashioned, with non-compound machinery. But in their own livery of grey hull and saloons, with red lining and red funnel with black top, they looked a picture and blended in with the marvellous scenery of the loch. *Prince George* did not sail after 1939, but *Princess May* soldiered on until 1951. *Prince Edward* was rather larger and fitted with compound machinery, and is seen here leaving Tarbet on a down service in the 1920s. She lasted until 1955. *Author's collection*

Below The end of a perfect day. Passengers disembark from *Waverley* at Craigendoran around 1928, while two crew members manoeuvre planks to deal with some deck cargo. On the bridge the captain supervises, while some passengers appear to be enjoying a bridge visit. Just behind him can be seen the traditional Clyde steamer destination indicator, consisting of individual slip boards projecting from a centre pole; this arrangement, which can also be seen on the pier, gave rise to the nickname of 'the fans' for destination boards, a name that continued to be used after this type was replaced by the more conventional framework, which is still used today. Also noticeable is the wire mesh that was fitted between the open rails of LNER steamers (and *King Edward*); this sensible arrangement must have prevented many a hat and toy from rolling off into the water.

Waverley was built in 1899 and modernised in 1919 and again in 1933, when shelters were placed fore and aft on the promenade deck. She was sunk by a bomb at Dunkirk in 1940 after putting up a very gallant fight and bringing down one of the attacking aircraft; many wounded soldiers were lost, but many were rescued, along with her master Captain Cameron who survived to take command of her successor in 1947. *Author's collection*

5. THE WESTERN ISLES

Oban and Mull

Not only is Oban an important transfer point between road, rail and steamer, but it is also a holiday resort in its own right. From around 1880 MacBrayne stationed several steamers at the port to provide local cruises, and thousands took advantage of these over the years until 1988, when the last (to Iona, by *Columba*) were withdrawn. However, rearrangement of the ferry schedules in the interests of rationalisation has in fact also had the effect of providing opportunities for day trips that were not previously possible, and in 1998 such cruises were offered to Coll and Tiree and to Colonsay, the latter being available on a Friday as an evening 'dine aboard' cruise, a three-course dinner being included in the fare. Menus now feature a range of dishes unknown on MacBrayne ships in the past. The ferry to Craignure on Mull also provides a chance to explore that island on a day-trip basis. But the cruise round Mull to Iona is now only possible on one day a year, when it is preformed by *Waverley*, and to many it is a matter of great regret that this most beautiful sail is no longer regularly offered.

One of the prettiest ships to have ever sailed out of Oban was *Grenadier* of 1885. She was built by J. & G. Thomson at Clydebank and fitted with what was by then obsolete oscillating engines; these were, however, compound and showed an economy of working compared to the simple-expansion engines of ships such as *Columba*. They also had the merit of being smooth in operation, a welcome feature on day trips. In 1902, when the ship was reboiled, her rather thin funnels were replaced by two of greater diameter and this improved her already elegant appearance. She features in the 'Para Handy' stories by Neil Munro, and that worthy was fond of comparing his 'puffer' to *Grenadier*, although for most people it would have required a considerable effort of imagination to see any similarity.

Although she sailed on various services and was also briefly a minesweeper from 1917 to 1919, *Grenadier* for most of her life ran the Staffa and Iona cruise from Oban in summer and the Clyde mail service to Ardrishaig in winter. On the former she must have become known to thousands from beyond Scotland. In this view she is at the North Pier in Oban on a summer morning, prior to working the Iona sailing in the early 1920s. *Author's collection*

Above The end of *Grenadier* was tragic and was one of the few fatal accidents to befall a Scottish steamer in the present century. Just before 1 am on the morning of 6 September 1927 she caught fire while lying at the North Pier. The blaze spread so rapidly that, by the time the fire brigade had arrived, it was clear that there was no chance of extinguishing it and the stern rope was therefore cut, to allow the ship to drift away from the pier and ultimately settle in the water. Some of the crew were saved only by jumping overboard and three did not survive. Among these was Captain A. McArthur, who had commanded *Grenadier* for many years and had been allowed to return for the 1927 season as an adviser to his successor. Perhaps he would have found it hard to survive the loss of his beloved ship. A local

stationer took several photographs of the damaged hulk, of which this is one.

Rebuilding of *Grenadier* was considered, but she was beyond economical repair and in 1928 the remains of the ship were towed to Ardrossan for scrapping. Her boilers were salvaged and saw further service in *Fusilier* and *Gondolier* respectively, and her figurehead was presented to the Glasgow Art Gallery for preservation. Not only was this a disaster in human terms, it was probably the last nail in the financial coffin of the old MacBrayne company, which had suffered the loss of three ships within four years, and contributed to its take-over by the LMS and Coast Lines in the following year.

Just visible behind *Grenadier* is the little screw steamer *Princess Louise* of 1898, which for many years ran short cruises from Oban under the ownership of Alexander Paterson. Her destinations were places such as Connell Ferry and Kerrera, and she was not really in competition with MacBrayne. She was bought by the larger firm in 1934 and thereafter sailed mostly out of Inverness, before being withdrawn in 1938. *Author's collection*

Left A much happier scene at the North Pier at the start of the summer season of 1974, as *King George V* prepares to embark passengers for Tobermory, Staffa and Iona. Her funnels have acquired the red lions rampant of Caledonian MacBrayne. By now the hour of departure had been put back to 10 am and the ship sailed on Monday, Tuesday, Thursday and Saturday via Tobermory and Staffa to arrive at the 'Sacred Isle' at 2 pm. Landing was by ferry and a ticket system ensured that those who went ashore first returned first, thus allowing everyone about 2 hours on the island. The ship sailed again at 4.30 pm and arrived back in Oban at 7. On Wednesday she started from Fort William and sailed direct from Oban, giving slightly less time ashore.

The Caledonian MacBrayne timetable was less eloquent than the pre-war MacBrayne guide, and merely said of Staffa, 'so colossal that it leaves you speechless'. But it still said firmly that the visit to Iona was 'not to be missed'.

Right In 1910 the last paddle steamer to be built for the MacBrayne fleet appeared from the yard of A. & J. Inglis, Pointhouse, Glasgow. Named *Mountaineer*, she was a relatively small ship and retained the open foredeck, by now obsolete in most fleets. However, an innovation was the enclosure of the forward part of the promenade deck by a solid bulwark, rather than an open rail. While this provided more shelter for passengers, it made the ship difficult to handle and in 1920 was replaced by the conventional rail.

The ship spent most of her career at Oban, working on the Crinan service after the loss of *Chevalier*, until it came to an end. She also relieved *Lochinvar* on the Mull service from time to time, and was often on the ferry service to Lismore. In between these runs she gave short summer cruises out of Oban to destinations such as Loch Sunart. But she did not seem to be successful and in 1938 was broken up at Port Glasgow. She is shown here backing out of Oban at some date after 1920. *Author's collection*

Below A much more successful vessel was *Lochinvar*. One of the earliest motorships for commercial service, she was built in 1908 by Scott & Sons of Bowling on the Clyde, and for almost all of her career (until 1955) she was used on the Sound of Mull service, the predecessor of the present Oban-Craignure ferry. The ship lay overnight at Tobermory and sailed at 7.45 am for Drimmin, Salen, Lochaline and Craignure, reaching Oban at 10.45, returning after the arrival of the morning train from Glasgow. Calls at Drimmin and Craignure were made by ferry and, when approaching, the ship's siren would give one blast if one ferryboat was required, or two if a pair would be needed. There were variations on certain days of the week or for special occasions, but the above basic schedule obtained for many years.

Lochinvar was no beauty, especially in her earlier years. She first had a tall, thin funnel right aft, which was later replaced by three separate exhaust pipes; in turn these were replaced by a small but more normal-looking funnel placed rather further forward. Cargo was handled by a crane situated amidships; this ugly but practical apparatus had to be given a goose-neck to clear the new funnel and thereafter could handle less weight than previously. But in all of her various guises, she was a supremely reliable ship and became a great favourite in Mull and Morvern. Under the command of Captain Malcolm Black in her later years, she seldom missed a sailing and only gales such as that of 31 January 1953 prevented her reaching Oban. This view shows her approaching Lochaline and its hotel in her second condition, probably be the mid-1920s. *Author's collection*

Above Today the hotel has reverted to private occupancy, the pier is derelict and the focus of activity has moved into the loch itself, the terminal of the car ferry from Fishnish on Mull. In May 1995 Caledonian MacBrayne's *Isle of Cumbrae*, built in 1976 for the Largs-Cumbrae service, sails out from the landing slip into Loch Aline.

Below Until she was required on the Clyde in summer from 1959, *Lochfyne* was the secondary cruise ship at Oban, sailing mainly to Fort William. However, in the 1960s she still returned north in May of each year to provide a combined programme of cruises for three weeks until the summer timetable came into operation, when *King George V*

came out and *Lochnevis* became the second cruise ship. On 21 May 1963 she had provided the Iona cruise via the south end of Mull, but a strong north-westerly gale was blowing and time at Iona was therefore cut short, as there was a risk of passengers not being able to reboard if she had lingered. Time ashore at Tobermory was given instead; as can be seen, it was still choppy even in the shelter of the bay and most passengers were glad to have solid ground under their feet again!

The small boat is MacBrayne's *Applecross*, built in 1944 and purchased in 1963 for the service from Kyle to Toscaig, but in 1965 relieving on the Tobermory-Mingary service. She then went to Iona as a ferry and was sold back to her original owner, a Mr Gibson, in 1969. She was re-acquired in 1973 and returned to Tobermory from 1981 to 1985, when she was again sold back to Mr Gibson. For a small ship she certainly had an involved history.

Below A very attractive postcard from 1931, *Lochfyne*'s first year in service, when she had a grey hull. She is shown, subject to some artistic licence, off Fingal's Cave on Staffa, while her passengers inspect the interior. In practice she would have anchored some way offshore. Landings here were always subject to the weather and could be dangerous; around 1930 two lady passengers were swept off the ledge and drowned. They ceased, as far as MacBrayne ships were concerned, in 1967, but can still be made by small boat from Iona or Mull. *Author's collection*

PLEASURE SAILINGS AND MOTOR EXCURSIONS
FROM OBAN

BY R.M.S. "LOCHFYNE"
(or other Steamer)

Weather and circumstances permitting

15th MAY TO 6th JUNE, 1964

DAVID MACBRAYNE LIMITED
STEAMER OFFICE, OBAN

Above King George V rests off Iona in 1974.

Left Cruising in the West Highlands has always been popular, and from 1947 to 1956 six- or 13-day cruises were provided from Liverpool and Ardrossan by Coast Lines Ltd, who used for this the former Irish Sea steamer *Patriotic* of 1912, renamed *Lady Killarney*. Originally she had a corn-coloured hull and funnel and looked like a miniature Orient liner, but these colours proved impracticable for Scottish service and she latterly had a black hull and the standard Coast Lines funnel. In 1955 it was still considered chic to express prices in guineas, and the 13-day cruises cost from 34 to 53 guineas (£35 14s to £55 13s). The ship is seen here alongside the Railway Pier at Oban in August 1952, with *Lochfyne* about to set off for Fort William from the North Pier. *Lady Killarney* went to the breakers after the 1956 season. Today similar cruises may be enjoyed in *Hebridean Princess*, formerly the MacBrayne car ferry *Columba*. *Author's collection*

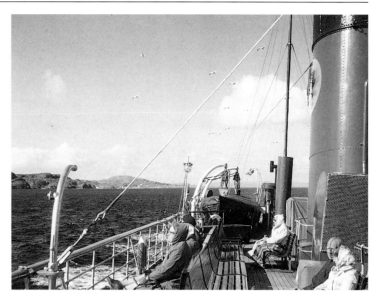

Looking back at Iona from the upper deck of *King George V* as she sets out for Oban via the south end of Mull in 1973, her second last summer on the cruise.

Over the sea to Skye

There have always been several sea routes to the Isle of Skye, including that made famous in song after the escape of Charles Edward Stuart from the Scottish mainland in 1746. Assuming that the words of the lyric are factual, he chose a more southerly route than that which will be considered here, namely the short crossing from Kyle of Lochalsh to Kyleakin.

It may seem odd to anyone who does not know the area, but Kyle of Lochalsh is in fact one of Britain's railway towns. There was very little there when, in 1896, the Highland Railway company extended its line from Strome Ferry to a point at the narrows of the Sound of Sleat, from which a short ferry trip brought one on to Skye. The reason for the extension had been to have sufficient space to build a terminus that would handle the increasing rail/steamer traffic and a harbour for the

The Highland Railway took over the ferry service between Kyle and Kyleakin in 1897, but leased its operation to private individuals. It was not a particularly lucrative business and various operators tried in vain to make it pay, using from 1914 motor launches that towed car and cattle barges as necessary. In the late 1920s, when the most recent of these gave up, the lease was taken by a Mr Clark, who had just arrived in the district. He introduced on the run the first boat to be fitted with a turntable, allowing it to load and unload at slipways and carry a few cars at a time; this ferry, *Kyleakin*, was introduced in 1930. The lease appears to have passed to MacBrayne in 1935, which held it for ten years,

Kyle Ferry and Station Hotel.

although the ferry boats were not considered part of the MacBrayne fleet. In this period a further two turntable ferries were put into service, *Moil* in 1936 and *Cuillin* in 1942.

This view, taken about 1925, shows operation in the days before the turntable ferries. A single car, probably a Darracq

12 or 15, is towed across by the launch *Skye* of 1922. Behind can be seen the hotel; this was originally a shooting lodge known as Kyle House and was virtually the only building in the place when the railway arrived. The HR bought it from its original owners and fitted it out as a comfortable, small hotel. *Author's collection*

LMS

KYLE OF LOCHALSH

By Norman Wilkinson, R.I.

Through, Glencarron, and along the shores of mighty Loch Carron, the LMS brings you to Lochalsh. All around is scenery of indescribable majesty, and only the narrow waters of the Kyle separate you from Skye. Among the islands of the western Scottish coast, and in the sea lochs of the Highlands, MacBraynes

steamers offer you a choice of many fascinating tours, from the Clyde in the south to the Hebrides in the north. And as a head quarters, what could be more desirable than the LMS Lochalsh Hotel, recently rebuilt and charmingly modern, yet in complete harmony with its surroundings.

Hotel Tariff and further information obtainable from Arthur Towle, Controller, LMS Hotel Services, St Pancras NW1.

For particulars of Steamboat Services apply to Messrs. David MacBrayne, 44, Robertson Street, Glasgow

In 1932-33 the LMS very considerably rebuilt the hotel, more than doubling its size, although publicity continued to refer to it as a 'comfortable small hotel' that was 'charmingly modern'. To increase business this poster was commissioned from Norman Wilkinson. Once again he used the technique of painting a distant view (from Kyleakin), although it has to be said that the prominence of the hotel is slightly exaggerated - while it is the largest building in Kyle, there is more to the rest of the town than the picture would suggest! The ship would appear to be MacBrayne's *Lochnevis* of 1934, which replaced *Fusilier* on the Mallaig-Kyle-Portree service in July of that year. A motor launch is crossing towards Skye, but there is no sign of any car ferry. *National Railway Museum, York*

fishing industry, rather than to reach the spot nearest to Skye. That link was then of little more than local importance, since given the state of roads on Skye most travellers used the steamer link to Rassay and Portree. It was only after 1930, when roads had improved enough to tempt the touring motorist and bus services had been started for those without cars, that the ferry began to see an increase in traffic. This growth continued unabated and the service required larger and larger ferries, culminating in *Loch Fyne* and *Loch Dunvegan* of 1991. Although that pair coped very well, the building of the privately operated bridge and the compulsory closure of the ferry on 16 October 1995 has ended the historic link. The ships have since been redeployed on other services.

Right Balanced precariously on one of the barges is a Rolls-Royce touring coach, belonging to Rankin Bros of Glasgow. This firm pioneered extended touring and advertised not only in the UK but also in North America. In the mid-1920s they operated the first inclusive tours from the Lowlands to Skye, and for these used Rolls-Royce cars, whose chassis had been extended by the firm of Mechan of Scotstoun, Glasgow. New bodywork, to accommodate 12 passengers, was fitted by Cadogan of Perth. *Robert Grieves Collection*

Below A slightly later view showing *Kyleakin* in action between 1931 and 1934. She has embarked a car at Kyle, but has no room for the queue of passengers, who will have to wait until the next sailing. Some may be wishing they had opted for the comfort of *Fusilier*, which is passing en route to Rassay and Portree. Just visible at the station pier is the bow of *Lochness*, built for the Stornoway service in 1929. *Author's collection*

Above A scene on the other side of the narrows around 1933. *Kyleakin* is again seen, as a tourer is coaxed aboard, while on the left passengers board a Dodge bus of the Skye Transport Company of Portree for that town. Serious competition for *Fusilier* has arrived on Skye! *G. E. Langmuir Collection, courtesy of The Mitchell Library, Glasgow City Libraries*

Below The LMS assumed direct control of the ferry on New Year's Day 1945. In post-war years traffic continued to grow at a great rate and new ships were regularly commissioned in an attempt to keep pace with the demands of the service. By 1970 there were five small ferries in operation, but all were replaced by two new and much larger 'drive through' ships, *Kyleakin* and *Lochalsh* in 1970-71. This is *Lochalsh* of 1957 at Kyle on 17 August 1961.

Finally even these two ships became inadequate for the traffic and two larger vessels were put into service in 1991. Named *Loch Fyne* and *Loch Dunvegan*, they had only a short though successful reign at Kyle and many local people would have been glad to see them continue in service, as an alternative to the bridge. In her last summer *Loch Dunvegan* sets off from Kyle on 16 May 1995, with the almost completed bridge in the background.

6. THE EAST COAST

Pleasure sailings had flourished on the east coast of Scotland in the years before 1914, when they came to a very abrupt end on the outbreak of war. They were not resumed immediately afterwards, as most of the ships had been lost and the piers had fallen into disrepair.

In the early 1920s anyone who fancied a sail in a full-sized ship (as opposed to a converted tug or a motor launch) had to make do with the 40-minute crossing from Granton to Burntisland, on which was operated, after minesweeping duties from 1917 to 1919, the veteran paddle ferry *William Muir*, which normally made six crossings of the Firth of Forth in each direction per day. She had been built at Kinghorn on the Forth in 1879 for the North British Railway, and when only two months old had carried the Dundee-bound passengers who were lost with the first Tay Bridge. However, she is best remembered as rebuilt in 1910 by Ramage & Ferguson of Leith; during this rebuild she was given a new engine, boilers and paddle wheels and the space thus saved was used to carry the increasing number of road vehicles. She emerged from the operation with one funnel in place of two, and this was now painted in the red/white/black of the North British Clyde steamers, instead of the previous black. She became something of an Edinburgh institution and there was great public regret when she was finally withdrawn early in 1937. Articles and poems were published in *The Scotsman* and other newspapers and seldom could so modest a ship have attracted such obituaries.

She was replaced by *Thane of Fife*, an ex-Mersey ferry, but she did not have the same following in the brief time that she served on the Forth. The Granton to Burntisland service was suspended in March 1940 and not resumed after the war was over. Attempts to revive it with car ferries in the 1950s and a catamaran in the 1990s have been equally unsuccessful.

Before 1914 non-landing returns to Burntisland were offered at an adult fare of 10d, and for many poorer people from Leith and Granton such excursions were the nearest they got to a holiday. It is not known if these fares were available again after 1919, but 'Wullie', as she was known locally, certainly retained her popularity for short trips. Returning from such an excursion around 1925, a group of passengers disembark at the slip in Granton harbour. *G. E. Langmuir Collection, courtesy of The Mitchell Library, Glasgow City Libraries*

As there seemed to be a demand for something more comfortable than the tugs with which the Grangemouth & Forth Towing Company had operated excursions since 1919, that company purchased in 1927 the steamer *Isle of Skye* from the Clyde, and she remained in service until 1939. Compared to pre-1914 days her programme was limited, being confined mainly to crossings to Aberdour and Kirkcaldy, with cruises upstream to the Forth (railway) Bridge. Occasional trips from the headquarters at Grangemouth were also made until 1934.

But despite the modest programme, *Fair Maid*, as she had now become, attracted a regular following and with 'music and dancing on board and teas and refreshments at shore prices' she was able to see off competition in the mid-1930s. Charter cruises, tendering work to visiting liners and relieving *William Muir* when the latter was off for overhaul kept her busy for much of the year. When war broke out, her sailings ceased and she returned to the Clyde in 1940.

An advantage gained by *Fair Maid* over any potential rivals in 1929 was the acquisition by the company of the lease of Hawcraig pier at Aberdour, which could be used at any state of the tide. However, as the old stone pier was more convenient for the town, she continued to use it when possible and is seen her landing a goodly crowd of excursionists in the late 1920s. Hawcraig pier can be seen beyond the steamer. *Author's collection*

Above *Fair Maid* was propelled by a single-crank compound engine, which imparted a distinct 'fore and aft' pulsating rhythm to her progress. It would appear that she was not fitted with electric light and the engine room staff had to work by the light of the large oil lamp suspended overhead. *Author's collection*

Below The saloon of *Fair Maid* was plain in the extreme, with none of the luxury then beginning to appear on the steamers on the Clyde, but probably sufficed for the short trips she undertook. *Author's collection*

Some competition was attempted in the years 1934-36 by the Redcliffe Shipping Company of Hull, who provided sailings, using the ex-MacBrayne ship *Fusilier* and, successively, two former Humber ferries. The second of these was *Brocklesby* of 1912, which was renamed *Highland Queen* and is seen here at Granton astern of *William Muir* in 1936, her second and last season on the Forth.

The sailings were variously advertised as 'Morrison's Firth of Forth Cruises' - G. Morrison being the local agent - and 'Queen Line Firth of Forth Cruises', and to a large extent they seemed to be planned to attract those who found the Scottish licensing laws somewhat restrictive; this applied particularly to the late Saturday cruise which left at 10 pm! Apart from Kirkcaldy, the Redcliffe ships did not call anywhere and often did not go anywhere in particular, but perhaps patrons did not mind about that. It is recorded that on one occasion *Highland Queen* was berthed by the master and a boy, the rest of the crew being quite incapable of action by the time she returned to base. The ships proved difficult to handle in the often exposed waters of the Forth and the sailings ended in the autumn of 1936. *G. E. Langmuir Collection, courtesy of The Mitchell Library, Glasgow City Libraries*

Above In view of the constant stream of traffic that now crosses the Forth Road Bridge, it is interesting to note that, in March 1951, *Mary Queen of Scots*, about to depart from Hawes Pier, South Queensferry, could comfortably accommodate all traffic on offer for her next sailing. By this time Messrs Denny, lessees of Queensferry Passage since 1934, were employing three diesel paddle vessels on the run, having added this ship in 1949 to replace the relief ship *Dundee*. At peak times she ran with her consorts *Robert the Bruce* and *Queen Margaret* of 1934, and a 20-minute frequency could be provided. Very soon after this photograph was taken, traffic began to grow by leaps and bounds, resulting in the building of a fourth ferry, *Sir William Wallace*, in 1956 and, in 1960, the decision to go ahead with the construction of the road bridge.

Below In 1960 pleasure cruising was resumed on the Forth by *The Second Snark*, the tug/tender normally employed by Messrs Denny at their shipyard in Dumbarton. She had been built there in 1938 and in many respects was a miniature version of *Countess of Breadalbane*, then sailing on Loch Awe. She became a popular little ship, offering cruises to view the road bridge under construction, as well as sailing from Granton in connection with Edinburgh Corporation Transport's city tours. The first pier of the road bridge can be seen in the background as she approaches Hawes Pier, South Queensferry, in August 1961.

When her owners went into liquidation in the autumn of 1963, *The Second Snark* was sold to Brown Brothers & Co for experimental work, but they continued the cruises for one more season. The vessel was subsequently purchased by Clyde Marine and as such is still engaged on cruising work on the Clyde.

One of the most interesting survivors among paddle steamers was the Tay ferry *B. L. Nairn*, which until 1966 was frequently to be found plodding between Dundee and Newport. She had been built at her home port by the Caledon Shipbuilding & Engineering Company for the Dundee Harbour Trust in 1929, and on the arrival of the second diesel screw ferry *Scotscraig* in the autumn of 1951 had officially been demoted to spare vessel, but in service on the Tay the Voith-Schneider propellers of the new ships gave much trouble and quite apart from covering overhaul periods, *B. L. Nairn* was in service for at least a few days in most months. Even as late as July 1965 she was for some days the only vessel on the crossing. By that time, however, her limited car capacity of 30 - compared with 60 on the newer ships - was a distinct drawback.

Named after the then Chairman of the Dundee Harbour Trust, the ferry was equipped with two sets of compound diagonal two-cylinder engines, one coupled to each paddle wheel. This made her extremely manoeuvrable and she could turn in her own length. The paddle wheels had an intriguing rhythm of 'THUMP, thump, thump, thump - pause - THUMP, thump, thump, thump', quite unfamiliar to anyone used to the continuous purring sound of *Jeanie Deans* running at speed, but, at a steady 6 knots, they got her across and back.

She was no beauty, but she was supremely reliable. Passengers had the shelter of a very spartan saloon, a smoke room with a permanent fug and a ladies' lounge. Although the Harbour Trust ran some cruises in the 1930s, there is no evidence that the *Nairn* was ever employed on these, but to many Dundonians a trip across the Firth on one of the 'Fifies' was always a welcome break, and she must have carried thousands seeking a brief escape from the city.

B. L. Nairn was laid up for a year after the opening of the road bridge in 1966, and would have been an ideal candidate for preservation along with the other ships that are now open to the public at Dundee. No one seems to have considered this, but there were plans to use her as a floating disco. Perhaps fortunately, these fell through and in the summer of 1967 she was towed away to Blyth for scrapping. In the first photograph she is shown at Newport on a wet afternoon in April 1966, with the outline of the bridge that would replace her just visible in the murk. The second shows a variety of cars seeking some shelter under her rather skimpy fo'c'sle while she paddles across the Tay.

When thinking of Scottish steamers, there is a temptation to consider only those ships that have operated on the West Coast. While services on the East Coast have certainly been more limited, rail and road having replaced many by the middle of the 19th century, it would be wrong to neglect mention of the fine ships that have operated for the North of Scotland, Orkney & Shetland Shipping Company Ltd, now part of the P&O Ferries group.

To replace *Saint Magnus* of 1924, the company unusually went to a Clyde yard and ordered *Saint Clair*, the third of that name, from the Ailsa Company of Troon. She was a motorship of 3,302 tons and by far the largest ship built for the company up to that time. She was launched on 29 February 1960 and went into service on the direct Aberdeen-Lerwick run in that summer. Her accommodation was thoroughly modern in design and she also had extensive deck space, with a particularly pleasant shade deck between the bridge and the funnel. Unfortunately she could also be considered a magnificent anachronism, since the car ferry era had already begun and she was the last large coastal passenger ship built for service in Britain. Cars still had to be craned aboard and the rate was expensive, £9 2s 6d return from Aberdeen to Lerwick for the smallest car at a time (1961) when the passenger return was only £6 10s.

However, *Saint Clair* proved to be a most popular ship. She made her last run in 1977 and was replaced by a car ferry of the same name. In this view she is discharging cargo at Matthew's Quay, Aberdeen, early on a January morning in 1967, after an overnight crossing from Lerwick.

No 164

ABERDEEN/LERWICK PASSENGER AND CAR SERVICE
North of Scotland, Orkney & Shetland Shipping Co. Ltd.
(Member of the P. & O. Group)

TRAVEL/MOTOR CAR TICKET

Right The North Company very actively promoted tourism and suggested that for a holiday that was completely different, few places could compare with Orkney and Shetland for a wide range of interests, healthy pleasure and varied charm. To encourage tourism further, the company acquired in 1902 the St Magnus Hotel at Hillswick on mainland Shetland, and for a brief period in the 1950s it also owned the Standing Stones Hotel at Stenness in Orkney. Based on these, and on other privately owned hotels, a variety of holidays was offered at very reasonable rates; in 1961 a 19/20-day holiday based on these two hotels could be enjoyed for a charge of £36 from Aberdeen.

This lunch menu of 1972 from the St Magnus Hotel depicts, with some licence, the steamer of the same name, which had been withdrawn in 1967. Built as *Saint Clair* in 1937, she was the first of the company's ships to be have a modern interior layout and a screened promenade below the bridge. She also served in northern waters during the war and returned safely. In 1960 she was renamed briefly *Saint Clair II*, then *Saint Magnus*, and served as such until rationalisation and withdrawal of passenger sailings to Leith made her redundant. She was the last coastal passenger steamer in service to be powered by reciprocating steam engines, which were exceptionally smooth-running. *Author's collection*

Below The habits of herring were of considerable importance to Scottish shipping companies since, while the fish themselves were caught by fishing boats, their movements entailed the simultaneous movement of those who dealt with them once landed, and the 'herring girls' were regular passengers in both MacBrayne and North of Scotland ships.

THE NORTH OF SCOTLAND ORKNEY & SHETLAND STEAM NAVIGATION CO LTD

MENU

LUNCHEON   75p

Tomato Juice
Oxtail Soup

Fried Haddock or Whiting

Creamed Potatoes
Garden Peas

Crunchy Cherry Pie with Cream
Strawberry Cream Dessert
Ice Cream with Raspberry
or Chocolate topping

Cheeseboard   10p

Coffee   10p

There was also a demand for barrels for the cured herring, and many of these were made by Messrs Dan Taylor & Sons, coopers and fish curers of Stonehaven, south of Aberdeen. To transport these barrels, two ships, *Halladale* and *Berriedale*, called at that tiny port regularly in the 1930s. The latter is seen here, loaded well above the gunwale with barrels; it is not clear if and how the crew were able to move around the ship! The location of the view has not been recorded, but it is clearly a large port, most probably Aberdeen. *James Craig*

7. THE NORTH ISLES

One of the last passenger/cargo services in Scotland was that from Lerwick to the North Isles of Shetland, which finally came to an end in 1975, thus terminating a tradition that stretched back to a time before the day of the steamer. In honesty, it should be said that after 1945 the passenger element came more and more to depend on holidaymakers making a round trip, rather than on travellers going from point to point, such passengers preferring the quicker route by bus and ferry, although these were not as yet car ferries. Another unusual feature of the route was that, for almost all of its existence, it was served by only two ships, both bearing the name *Earl of Zetland*.

The first *Earl* was a most remarkable ship, built in 1877 at Paisley by John Fullerton & Company to the order of the Shetland Islands Steam Navigation Company, which merged with the North of Scotland, Orkney & Shetland Shipping Company Ltd in 1890. She served the North Isles faithfully until August 1939, when, amid celebrations tinged with a good deal of sadness, she was replaced by the second *Earl* and departed for Aberdeen and, it was assumed, the scrapyard. However, just five months later she was back, her successor being required on the Pentland Firth run to Orkney and she continued on her old route until June 1946. Then for a second time she cheated the breakers and went off to the Middle East to carry immigrants to Palestine, as *Yehuda Halevy*, and was finally broken up at Haifa in 1948.

The second *Earl* was a smart motorship built by Hall, Russell & Company of Aberdeen, and finally took up permanent duty on the service in June 1946. She had excellent accommodation for a ship of her size, but in a sense she came too late; roads had been improved during the war and bus transport had developed. For local people she was primarily a cargo steamer, and many tourists enjoyed her facilities on round trips from Lerwick, which were energetically promoted by the North Company, all 'in pursuit of a life far from the bustle and tiring pressure of great cities', as the guide phrased it.

In her later years the timetable provided for two departures per week at 8 am on Monday and Friday from Lerwick to Baltasound on Unst, the most northerly island, with different calls at intermediate ports. As the actual times at these ports depended on cargo requirements, passengers usually had the chance to go ashore where there was a pier; at many places, transhipment still depended on a 'flit' boat, although this was now a motor launch rather than the oared 'sixareen' of the past. Arrival time at Baltasound therefore varied, but was seldom before 5 pm. Round trip passengers could sleep on board, in compact but comfortable cabins.

Earl of Zetland returned south on the following day, normally, unless it was the time of the lamb sales, with a much quicker passage, arriving in Lerwick just after lunchtime. The Wednesday sailing went only as far as Mid Yell, and was offered as a day trip from Lerwick, at a fare in 1961 of 25 shillings, including lunch. The Friday departure made a good connection with a ship arriving from the south.

The North Isles trip featured in some of the inclusive package tours offered by the company, and for passengers on these a bus tour was available on Unst to allow them to view Muckle Flugga, the most northerly point of the British Isles. It made a most interesting if leisurely experience and many were sorry when *Earl of Zetland* made her last sailing in February 1975. No doubt the buses and the present-day ferries of Shetland Council offer a quicker and more efficient service, but there is less chance to catch a glimpse of local life and of the fine coastal scenery and sea-bird life that lay along the route of the North Isles ship. *Earl of Zetland*, like her predecessor, evaded the breakers and is now a restaurant ship in London. The following photographs were taken on a voyage from Lerwick to Baltasound on *Earl of Zetland* in May 1972.

Above Returning from a round voyage, *Earl of Zetland* glides into her berth at the Victoria Pier at Lerwick, with a large Russian trawler on the left.

Below Although containerisation had been introduced on the company's services from the Scottish mainland, it did not operate north of Lerwick and cargo for the North Isles had to be handled on an individual basis. A container has been opened and a box of Mitchell & Muil's Sponge Delicacies is being carefully manoeuvred aboard the *Earl*. Mitchell & Muil ran a restaurant and bakery business in Aberdeen and their products were much enjoyed throughout the north-east.

Above The first port of call on the Friday sailing was Whalsay, where there was ample time to go ashore and discover this former W. Alexander Bedford coach, which had been converted to a mobile shop, and the vintage petrol pumps. *Earl of Zetland* discharges cargo at the pier beyond.

Below At Mid Yell another long call was made, again allowing time ashore. Now the *Earl* is framed between stacks of peat.

Above By the time she departs it is difficult to see the pier for the cargo! Tetley's teabags, Zip fire-lighters and Carnation milk seem to figure largely, and the pier staff look as though they did not know where to make a start.

Right Where there was no pier, as at Uyeasound, a motor launch came out to meet the *Earl*, and cargo and passengers were transhipped. To begin with it is a case of 'pass the parcel'.

By the time the cargo has been stowed there is little room for the passengers, but eventually all are safely aboard and the ferry can cast off.

Above Rounding the east coast of Unst, the ship is exposed to the full force of the North Sea, but *Earl of Zetland* was a good sea boat and most passengers found her motion not unpleasant.

Below Finally she is safely alongside at Baltasound, sharing the pier with many fishing boats, and passengers can go ashore to enjoy the comforts of the local hotel, or take a bus trip to peer at Muckle Flugga lighthouse through the rain.

The alternative route to the North Isles was by bus and ferry, as seen in this scene at Ulsta on Yell in 1957. The ferry *Shalder*, a converted fishing boat, has just arrived from Toft on the Shetland mainland and passengers are transferring to and from the waiting Bedford buses of W. Sandwick Motors. That on the left has Mulliner bodywork, while AGS 676 on the right has a 19-seater body by SMT. A car and Bedford van complete the picture. Covered accommodation on *Shalder* was limited, and on a wet day the crossing, though short, must have been most uncomfortable. *Robert Grieves Collection*

8. STEAMERS IN EXILE

There has been a long tradition of Scottish steamers leaving their native waters for service elsewhere. Even in the first decade of steamboat operation, Clyde steamers went abroad and there is a record of *Elizabeth*, the second steamer to be built, being transferred to Liverpool. Another early steamer went to France and was reported to be running on the Seine in 1817. Probably the greatest exodus was caused by the American Civil War, when so many fast paddle steamers were purchased by the agents of the 'Emperor of China' (in reality the Confederate Government) that in 1863 there were hardly enough boats left to maintain the summer services. While most of the blockade runners had short, if

romantic, careers, one at least, *Star*, was recorded as still being afloat at Nassau in the Bahamas in 1922. In later years most ships that were sold from Scottish waters were past their best, and their subsequent careers tended to be short and usually unsuccessful, apart from the members of the 'Maid' Class of 1953 that went to Greece and Italy and now have served longer in their new homes than they did on the Clyde.

Princess Patricia, ex-Queen Alexandra (1902)

Following the success of *King Edward*, the Turbine Steamer Syndicate Ltd ordered an improved

Princess Patricia alongside the CPS pier in Victoria. On the other side can be seen the three funnels of either *Princess Kathleen* or *Princess Marguerite*, both built on the Clyde in 1925 for the Vancouver-Victoria-Seattle Triangular Route, and beyond the steamers can be seen part of the roof of the Empress Hotel, perhaps the most

famous of all the Canadian Pacific hotels. With the white paint once again extended down to main deck level and her yellow, black-topped funnels, *Princess Patricia* could easily be mistaken for a Clyde turbine, although the awning on the promenade deck aft would have been a novel feature. *A. Duncan*

version from Messrs Denny and this ship appeared in 1902 as *Queen Alexandra*. She was even faster than the pioneer turbine, having attained 21.95 knots on trial, but astern power was somewhat lacking. After spending a week sailing out of Oban, she settled down on the Campbeltown service until September 1911, when fire broke out while she was tied up at Greenock. The damage looked serious, the upperworks and saloon being destroyed, but on closer inspection it appeared that it was entirely superficial and that the hull and machinery had not been harmed. Nevertheless, the owners decided to take advantage of the situation to order a new ship with certain improvements, and *Queen Alexandra* was sold to the British Columbia Coast Service of Canadian Pacific Steamships, who had already expressed interest before the fire.

Having been repaired by her builders and fitted with an enclosed saloon amidships on the promenade deck, the ship was renamed *Princess Patricia* after the daughter of the Duke of Connaught, who had just become Governor General of Canada. She left the Clyde on 17 January 1912 and, after what her chief engineer, Walter Anderson, called 'an awful voyage', reached Victoria safely on 18 March. The actual steaming time had been 43 days, and it says a great deal for the sound construction of the ship that she coped so well; there had been times on the voyage when the bow and stern had been suspended between two Atlantic rollers, and those on board had feared that she would break her back. The Captain returned to Scotland after delivery, but Mr Anderson chose to stay with the ship and served on board throughout her career in Canada.

After overhaul to repair storm damage and conversion to burn oil, Princess Patricia entered service on the Vancouver-Nanaimo run on 11 May and thus began a most successful second career. Her speed allowed her to complete the passage in 2 hours, although the schedule required only 2¼, and as this was a very great improvement on the ship previously used, which could manage 12 knots with luck, users of the service were delighted with the 'Pat', as she became known in Canada. There were no intermediate calls on this service and the lack of astern power was less of a drawback than it had been on the Clyde.

However, as automobile traffic developed, her lack of space for this became a disadvantage and she was replaced on the service in 1928 by another Clyde-built ship, *Princess Elaine*, a product of John Brown's yard. *Princess Patricia*'s hull and machinery were nevertheless as good as new, and for some years she was used as an excursion and relief ship, but was laid up from 1932. In late 1935 she became a floating boarding house during a waterfront strike in Vancouver, a humiliating role for a fine ship. Finally she was scrapped at Victoria early in 1937. Many in British Columbia were sad to see the end of the dashing and pretty little 'Pat', and her bell was presented to the City of Nanaimo to mark her long association with it.

Anzio I, ex-*Lochinvar*

One of the most tragic stories is that of this doughty little MacBrayne motorship. Having been a spare boat for some years, she finished her Scottish career on her old run to the Sound of Mull from Oban on Saturday 28 May 1960. Rather surprisingly in view of her age – she was built in 1908 – and her very active life, she was at once purchased for further service by Timbercraft of Shandon on the Gareloch, who resold her to a Mr C. Harvey. He had in 1960 run a service between Sheerness and Southend with *Anzio*, an ex-RN 'Fairmile' motor launch, and this had proved very successful. There may have been some idea of running *Lochinvar* out of Brighton, since she briefly carried the name *Brighton Belle*, but in the event the first *Anzio* was sold and she took up service on the Thames under the name *Anzio I* in 1961. At first she retained her crane, but this was removed in 1963. She was well run and carried good loads, but the redevelopment of Sheerness harbour deprived her of a berth and she did not sail after that year.

Two years of lay-up followed and it was even more of a surprise when in 1966 she was sold for yet further service, to Cromarty Cruises Ltd, who intended to run her from Inverness. She set out for her new home on 1 April 1966, but on the following day was overwhelmed by a storm off the mouth of the Humber and was driven ashore near Cleethorpes. Despite valiant efforts by those on shore, it proved to be impossible to get a line aboard; her crew all perished and the sea soon dealt with the hulk. It was a sad end to a long and happy career.

Anzio I being followed into Southend by Medway Queen in September 1963, shortly before the end of the careers of both ships. Medway Queen, after a period of exile in the Isle of Wight, is now happily back in her old haunts and is being restored by members of the trust that bears her name.

Marchioness of Graham

The advent of the car ferry Glen Sannox in mid-1957 deprived this turbine steamer of her employment serving Arran and, after a season of not very successful cruising, she was laid up in the Alber Harbour in Greenock. In the following year she was sold to a Greek owner, Nicholas Diapoulis, and left the Clyde early in 1959, her saloon windows boarded up and bags of coal stowed in every conceivable corner. For the voyage out she was probably renamed Theo and had a blue band added to her funnel.

On arrival in Greece she was immediately converted to diesel power and was greatly altered, both internally and externally. This was the time of the beginning of mass tourism and the 'fly cruise' concept, and Greek shipowners bought up many redundant coastal and cross-channel vessels to tap the new market. But although Hellas, as ship had now become, looked streamlined and modern and even boasted a tiny swimming pool, she was, despite lengthening to 245 feet, still essentially a ship designed for short voyages, and she must have seemed somewhat cramped to those cruising in her for trips of several days' duration.

An artist's impression of New Hellas, ex-Marchioness of Graham, during her cruising days. The caption on the reverse calls her 'The Empress of Cruise Yachts'. Author's collection

In 1963 she was renamed *Nea Hellas* and in the following year was chartered to the Kavounides Shipping Company and renamed *Galaxias*. In 1966 she was sold again, this time to Delphi Cruises SA, and renamed *El Greco*. She was now used on two- and five-day cruises around the Greek islands, and is also reported to have sailed from Barcelona to the Balearics. Early in 1968 she was laid up near Peiraeus, and did not sail again. She lay at her berth for eight years, becoming more and more rusty and unkempt, and also had to suffer the indignity of being arrested for debt. Finally the shipbreakers put her out of her misery.

It would seem that none of her cruising ventures was successful enough to last for long, probably because she was essentially too small for the routes concerned. It was a sad postscript to a successful Clyde career and she deserved better.

Queen of the South, ex-Jeanie Deans

Steamer enthusiasts were delighted to learn late in 1965 that the laid-up *Jeanie Deans* had been sold

Queen of the South laid up in the Pool of London in July 1966. This was still then a working harbour, as the numerous cranes testify.

for further service on the Thames, having been bought by a concern known as the Coastal Steam Packet Company Ltd. On her first attempt to leave the firth, she developed paddle wheel trouble and it seemed that she was, as one newspaper put it, 'sweirt tae gang' (reluctant to go). Finally she did leave on 5 November 1965 and arrived safely in the Thames nine days later. She was reconditioned and painted in an approximation of her LNER livery and externally looked very fine. Internally it was a different matter, and she suffered from serious mechanical failures that effectively limited her 1966 sailings to eight days in all, and some of these ended prematurely.

But this was not to be the end. More money was spent on her during the winter of 1966/67. Her boiler was retubed, the dining saloon and lounge were totally renovated and she was given a bow rudder. But her boiler was still liable to failure and her first cruise of the 1967 season consisted of being towed to a buoy off Tower Pier. She did begin sailing on Saturday 24 June and managed to continue until Wednesday 12 July, when paddle

Beyond the ship can be seen the old London Bridge, soon afterwards replaced by the present structure and sold for re-erection in the USA.

At the end of one of her successful trips, *Queen of the South* backs away from Greenwich pier on the evening of Saturday 1 July 1967. On the north bank are many derelict properties, in an area since transformed by the rebuilding of Docklands.

wheel damage, soon compounded by boiler trouble, ended her second season. She was laid up and at the end of the year sold for scrapping in Belgium.

It was a great pity that the Thames venture did not meet with more success, especially for those who had put much money, time and enthusiasm into the plans. She had the river to herself in 1967, the GSN motorships having been withdrawn, and given a little more luck could have done well. But perhaps the new *Queen* was rather past her prime, and the days when Londoners flocked to take a sea trip to 'Margate, Ramsgate or the Essex Coast' had already passed by 1966. Perhaps the only good to come of it all was that lessons were learned that were later applied to the very successful running of *Waverley* on her present basis.

Lochiel

A ship whose fate hung in the balance as this book was being written was the former MacBrayne motor vessel *Lochiel*. She was the fifth of the modern motorships built for the company before the Second World War and was commissioned in 1939 for the Islay service, although she spent her first season on cruises from Oban. Once dredging work had been completed at West Loch Tarbert, she took up her intended station and remained on it until 1970, the only breaks being occasional relief work on the Clyde and several months in the autumn of 1960, when she ran aground and sank in the West Loch.

She was replaced by the car ferry *Arran* from the Clyde and was sold to a company who optimistically tried to use her on day excursions from Fleetwood to Douglas. As her average passage time was 6 hours, this was unsuccessful. After being at various ports in the West Country, she went to Bristol as a floating restaurant in 1978, and for some time was a popular and well-run venue in the city. She changed hands several times and finally fell into disuse. Despite some heroic last-minute attempts to save this fine Denny-built motorship, the last traditional

Lochiel serving as a floating restaurant in Bristol. *Miss G. Crewe*

MacBrayne ship afloat, she went to the breakers at the end of 1995. The saga again emphasised the impossibility of guaranteeing preservation of a ship that has been sold for static use, and the complete lack of official interest in this aspect of Britain's maritime heritage.

9. CIGARETTE CARDS

Ever since postcards came into use, in the first years of this century, they have depicted Scottish steamers, and these have been avidly collected by generations of enthusiasts. Less well known, however, is the series of cigarette cards 'River and Coastal Steamers' issued by the Glasgow firm of Stephen Mitchell & Son, who manufactured cigarettes in a factory in the east end of the city. The craze for collecting such cards was at its height in the period between the wars, and no doubt many contemporary ship-lovers smoked more than they should have done in an effort to complete the set of 70.

The ships on the cards are well drawn and the colouring is generally good, save where white funnels come out slightly pink. A wide range of Scottish steamers is covered, but many from English waters are also featured. There are quite a few Clyde steamers, although strangely none of the LNER fleet is illustrated. Nor is *King George V* included, although the turbine *Glen Sannox* is, suggesting that the set first appeared in early 1926; it is not known how long it remained in circulation. As far as is known, the only other Clyde steamer to feature on a cigarette card was *Columba*, which was one of a set of 'Famous Ships' issued by Wills, but in comparison with the Mitchell set it is a rather poor illustration of the ship in her early condition.

Five steamers have been chosen from the set, three from the East Coast, as a reminder that, until 1939, there was a flourishing and very popular series of passenger services operated between Scottish East Coast ports and London. The other two remember Scotland's holiday connections with the Isle of Man.

The cards are reproduced here slightly larger than actual size.

The first card of the set depicts the steamer *Aberdonian* of the Aberdeen Steam Navigation Company, a ship of 1,648 tons. She had been built in 1909 at Glasgow by D. & W. Henderson & Company and remained in service until 1939, latterly in partnership with *Lochnagar*. She sailed from Aberdeen every Tuesday and from London every Saturday, the trip taking around 36 hours. *Aberdonian* carried 80 passengers in 1st Class and 120 in 2nd. The passenger service was not resumed after the Second World War and she was sold for service in the Far East, being ultimately broken up in India.

The Dundee, Perth & London Shipping Company traded between the first and last ports in its title until 1967, but did not carry passengers after 1939. No 49 of the series depicts its steamer *Perth*, built in 1915 at Dundee by the Caledon Shipbuilding & Engineering Company. She immediately went into service as an armed patrol ship, then took up civilian duties in 1919. Accommodation seems to have been rather more elaborate than on the Aberdeen Company's ships, since the card mentions private suites on the upper bridge deck, music and smoke rooms, and baths. The steamer left Dundee each Saturday and London each Wednesday, the average passage time taken being 36 hours. *Perth* was later sold to the Falklands Islands Company, then to Italy, and was finally scrapped in 1962.

Top The London & Edinburgh Shipping Company ran a thrice-weekly service between Leith and London, using in the inter-war years the steamers *Royal Fusilier* of 1924 - the subject of card No 56 - *Royal Archer* of 1928 and *Royal Scot* of 1930. The last of these carried only 12 passengers, but *Royal Fusilier* had accommodation for 160 in 1st Class and 200 in 2nd. For the former there were staterooms on the bridge deck for two, three and four people, a music room and a smoke room, as well as hot and cold water baths. The ship was built by the Caledon Company of Dundee, and was lost by air attack in the Irish Sea in 1940.

Middle Until about 1970 one of the favourite holiday destinations of Glaswegians was the Isle of Man, and it was therefore appropriate that card No 63 should have shown the Isle of Man Steam Packet Company's *Snaefell*, which frequently sailed from Ardrossan to Douglas. She had been built by Fairfield in 1906 as *Viper* for the Ardrossan-Belfast daylight service of Messrs G. & J. Burns, and rapidly became very popular, thanks to her speed of 22 knots and the quality of her accommodation. She resumed service in 1919 but the Irish troubles killed the daylight sailing's holiday traffic and she was sold in 1920 to the Manx company. She was then used on a variety of services and was one of the two ships left to the company to keep services running during the Second World War. By the time peace returned, she was worn out and was sold in the summer of 1945 to be broken up at Port Glasgow. This did not actually happen for a further three years, and the battered grey hull and red funnels became in the meantime something of a local landmark.

Bottom The last card in the set, No 70, depicted *Yarrow*, one of the few ships associated with the Isle of Man not to have been owned by the Steam Packet Company. Strictly speaking she was not a Scottish steamer, but for many years from 1863 the North British Railway's subsidiary Steam Packet Company had maintained a service from the railway port of Silloth on the Solway Firth to Dublin and, in summer, Douglas; until 1919 there was also a service to Liverpool. From 1892 the services were jointly owned by the NBR and William Sloan & Company, the latter actually managing the service. *Yarrow* was very similar to their Clyde ships.

She sailed two or three times each week from Silloth, usually around 6 pm, and rail connections and through fares were advertised from Glasgow, Edinburgh and Newcastle. Calls at Douglas were made in summer only, and most of these were advertised as being for passengers only; as the time of arrival and departure at that port was normally between midnight and 3 am, it would not have seemed to be particularly convenient. Peel was used if Douglas was unapproachable.

In 1929 Sloan's share of the service was acquired by Palgrave, Murphy & Company, shipowners of Dublin, and *Yarrow* was renamed *Assaroe*, after a waterfall in County Donegal; her funnel colouring became yellow with a green band and black top. The service ended with the outbreak of war and was not resumed in 1945, *Assaroe* being broken up two years later.

Cards from the author's collection.

The last word

Caledonian MacBrayne's latest ferry, *Clansman*, at Brodick in January 1999.

BIBLIOGRAPHY

There is now an extensive literature on Scottish steamers, from which the following works have been consulted in the preparation of this book:

Brodie, Ian *Steamers of the Forth* (David & Charles, 1976)

Coton, Richard H. *A Decline of the Paddle Steamer* (Paddle Steamer Preservation Society, 1971)

Donaldson, Gordon *Northwards by Sea* (Donaldson, no date)

Duckworth, C. L. D., and Langmuir, G. E. *Clyde River and Other Steamers*, 4th ed (Brown, Son & Ferguson, 1990)

Clyde and Other Coastal Steamers, 2nd ed (T. Stephenson & Sons, 1977)

Railway and Other Steamers, 1st ed (Shipping Histories, 1948)

West Highland Steamers, 2nd ed (Richard Tilling, 1950)

Fraser, Chris *Christie Boy* (Fraser & Son, 1994)

Grimshaw, G. *British Pleasure Steamers* (Richard Tilling, 1945)

Hacking, Norman R. and Kaye Lamb, W. *The Princess Story* (Mitchell Press Ltd, 1974)

Haws, Duncan *Merchant Fleets – Britain's Railway Steamers, Scottish and Irish Companies* (TCL Publications, 1994)

Lyon, David J. (ed) *The Denny List* (National Maritime Museum, 1975)

MacArthur, I. C. *The Caledonian Steam Packet Company* (Clyde River Steamer Club, 1971)

MacBrayne Centenary, 1851-1951 (D. MacBrayne, 1951)

MacBraynes for the Highlands (Albion Vehicle Preservation Trust, 1977)

McCrorie, I. and Monteith, Joy *Clyde Piers – a pictorial record* (Inverclyde District Libraries, 1982)

McDonald, Dan *The Clyde Puffer* (David & Charles, 1977)

MacHaffie, F. G. *Jeanie Deans 1931-1967* (Jeanie Deans Publications, 1977)

Meek, D. *An T-Aiseag an Iar* (Pollock & Co, 1977)

Paterson, Alan J. S. *Classic Scottish Paddle Steamers* (David & Charles, 1982)

Robson, Adam *The Saga of a Ship, The Earl of Zetland* (Shetland Times, 1982)

Thomas, John *G&SW Steamers in LMS days* (unpublished manuscript)

Thornton, E. C. B. *Thames Coast Pleasure Steamers* (T. Stephenson & Sons, no date, but c1970)

Turner, Robert D. *The Pacific Princesses* (Sono Nis Press, 1977)

Walls, J. and Hamilton G. *The Renfrew Ferry* (Renfrew Historical Society, 1984)

Whittle, John *Speed Bonny Boat, the story of Caledonian MacBrayne Ltd, 1969-1990* (Saltire Communications, 1990)

Williamson, Capt James *Clyde Passenger Steamers, 1812-1901*, facsimile edition (SPA Books, 1977)

Wilson, Roy *Passenger Steamers of the Glasgow and South Western Railway* (Twelveheads Press, 1991)

LMS and LNER Holiday Guides, various years

MacBrayne Holiday Guides, 1934 and 1936

Dunoon & Rothesay Holiday Guides, various years

LMS, LNER, MacBrayne, Williamson-Buchanan, British Railways, North of Scotland Shipping Co timetables, various years

Ship Ahoy, quarterly journal of the World Ship Society, South Wales Branch, 1960-1969

Sea Breezes, various issues

Ships Monthly, various issues

INDEX